BROKE COLLEGE KIDS' GUIDE TO FINANCIAL SUCCESS

DR. CLEMENT OGUNYEMI,
The Finance Doctor®

Broke College Kids' Guide to Financial Success
By: Dr. Clement Ogunyemi, The Finance Doctor®
ISBN: 979-8-218-53084-6

Editor: Grammargal@Fiverr
Cover and Layout: JBookDesigns@Fiverr

DEDICATION

This book is dedicated to every young person who dares to dream big, like me. To every young person who, like me, just wants to create a solid financial future for themselves and for many generations after them. Lastly, this book is dedicated to every kid whose financial situation may have led them to believe that college was not possible for them. This one is for each of you. Continue marching onward and upward, and never stop believing in your dreams!

ACKNOWLEDGMENTS

Where do I even start? When I first set out on this journey, it was to ensure that everyone within my circle had the tools to achieve financial freedom and live comfortably. My family can tell you that anytime I went to an internship, seminar, or continuing education course or just watched CNBC, they would get flooded with new information! Most people don't realize how draining it can be to pour your heart and soul into your work, your teachings, and writing books like this one. I have been beyond blessed to have an extremely strong, tight support system, who continue to lift me up and push me forward. Even when frustration sets in and I have considered quitting, I remember my *why*. Alyssia, Latoya, Joshua, Olaolu, Daniel, thank you all so much for being my original *why*. To my parents, who have always pushed me to greatness and loved me unconditionally when I made mistakes, thank you. Thank you for instilling the value of hard work and perseverance. To my love, MJ, thank you for putting up with the late nights, grumpy mornings, frustrations, etc. It has not gone unnoticed, and I will forever be grateful. To my kiddos, Ethan, Aiden, and new baby O, I will never stop fighting for your future and will always make sure you are good!

PREFACE

CONGRATULATIONS!

You have taken the first steps in achieving your financial freedom and becoming a financially literate individual or family. It is my pleasure to be able to guide you through this process and provide you with the tools necessary to make it to the end of your journey. I hope that by the end of this book, you can take these principles and concepts and apply them to your daily life. More importantly, I hope your financial health will be improved and that you move from the death grips of debt and poor financial decision-making to a worry-free life of financial freedom.

Like you, when I began my financial literacy journey, I felt extremely overwhelmed (helpless even) and honestly did not see a way out. I knew absolutely *nothing* about what it took to be financially free. I thought that if I could just make more money, then my finances would automatically be fixed. But do you want to know a secret? It is **okay** and you **can** do it!

Dream big, but also put **action** to those dreams.

DO NOT READ THIS BOOK IF ANY OF THE FOLLOWING APPLIES:

- You plan to make **excuses** for not fixing your financial situation.

- You are **not** willing to take **action**.

- You already know **everything** about money.

If you do not fall into any of the three above categories, then please continue reading!

Yours Truly,

Dr. Clement O. Ogunyemi
The Finance Doctor ®

CONTENTS

BEFORE WE GET STARTED: MINDSET MATTERS

If you want to be a winner, then stop
doing the things losers do . . .

When we think about mindset, we often discuss the 80/20 rule. This rule applies to our money mindset as well. Reclaiming control of your money is **20% knowledge and 80% behavior**. Think about it. You can have all the knowledge in the world, but if you do not put action to that knowledge, then it is knowledge wasted.

I will gladly provide you with the 20% right here within this book. But no matter how much step-by-step knowledge I provide, it is up to you to apply this to your everyday life. The blueprint is right here, but none of it matters if you don't enter this with the right mindset. Understand this: there will be many ups and downs along your journey to financial freedom and independence, and there will be some failures along the way. However, what separates the wealthy from the not so wealthy is how they approach failure. Will you quit, or will you look at that failure as a lesson learned? Will you tell yourself that financial freedom is too hard, or will you keep pushing toward that vision?

In the words of a great philosopher (Dory from *Finding Nemo*), you have to "just keep swimming." Even when things get dark and scary, you have to just . . . keep . . . swimming. There will be days when self-doubt creeps in. There will be days when you find yourself falling back into old habits. There will be days when you feel like giving up is the easier option. I would be a liar if I told you that this road is as smooth as a baby's bottom. But the thing about it is, if this road were easy, then everyone would be wealthy, right? No one would need a Harvard education or need to spend tens of thousands of dollars on a formal education.

What I can tell you is that the satisfaction of reaching all your goals is worth the temporary discomfort. The gratification of changing your family's future is worth the dynamic mindset shift. Start to see yourself financially free! Start to see yourself wealthy. Start to see yourself creating generational wealth. Start to see yourself breaking generational curses. See yourself helping those around you. This is what a true mindset shift looks like: knowing that you are worthy of achieving freedom and that you can and will get there!

I know that as some of you are reading this text, you are thinking to yourself, "I can try my best to do these things." I will ask you, like I always ask my kids and any adult I speak with about their goals, "Are you a try-er, or are you a do-er?" You see, as long as you just "try," then that is all you have conditioned your mind to do . . . try. But when you start to condition yourself as a do-er, you begin to shift your mindset into truly finding ways to achieve what you set out to do, instead of quitting after you "tried." The fact that you have spent the money to buy this book and are taking the time to read it lets me know that you are willing to be a do-er and not just someone who says, "Oh well, I tried."

You must live like no one else (today), so
that you can live like no one else (later).
—Dave Ramsey

You must also be comfortable with being uncomfortable. Yes, this sounds beyond cliché, but it is true, and I can tell you firsthand how well it works. When I was in college, I was okay with missing out on a few parties in order to work an extra shift and make some additional income so I could achieve my goal at the time, buying a house and a car while still in college. And guess what? I did just that! I was comfortable being uncomfortable and maybe missing out on a few things in order to achieve my goals and dreams. I bought my first house a week after my twenty-first birthday (and that is only because I almost got cold feet and stalled the closing). I kept that house for close to twenty years and rented it out for the majority of that time, then sold it for a profit. One of my favorite quotes is from Dave Ramsey, in which he states, "You have to live like no one else (today) so that you can live like no one else (later)." I am not saying that I never went to parties during college, but there were many times when I simply declined the invitation because I knew what my mission was and refused to let anything stop me.

I don't tell you these things to brag on myself. On the contrary, I tell you these things to show you that you *can* do it. I am just a kid from Grambling, Louisiana, who dared to dream big and act on my dreams. I'm just a kid who dared to go against the grain and figure this money thing out. My friends who have known me long enough will tell you that I am bold enough to openly share these money "secrets" with anyone who will listen.

Don't be afraid to celebrate small wins. It is okay and can give you the motivation necessary to push forward!

I will leave you with this: **Write down your visions and make them clear for yourself.** Make them concrete and put them somewhere where they stay top of mind. There is something about writing down your goals and aspirations that makes them real to you. People who write down their goals are 33% more successful in achieving them than those who just formulated those outcomes in their heads.

I make it a point to sit down with my family to do annual vision boards. I make sure they understand that their goals not only need to be concrete but also be measurable and realistic. I will not say that I will make $1 billion in the next twelve months if I have not even made a plan to make $100,000. Making $1 billion is a big and probably attainable dream, but how realistic is it in that scenario? As you go through this process, I want you to remember that you usually have to crawl before you can walk, but anything you set your mind to is within your reach.

INTRODUCTION

So, you have walked across that stage. You are officially a high school graduate. You have your college acceptance letter(s) in hand and have chosen the school you will have an absolute blast at over the next four (and sometimes five or six) years of your life! You celebrate your first summer as a high school graduate. Now it is time to go shop for a new fit, get a fresh haircut (or doo), and head to the registrar and financial aid. Yay, you are officially registered for a couple of classes. Time to get those forty-pound books that your professor says you "absolutely cannot pass their class without."

You walk into the bookstore and select your first book: $500 for one book? How ever will you be able to pay for that? Just then, you realize that you have signed up for the requisite twelve credit hours for that semester! That's three more classes! After doing some very quick math, you realize that one semester of books alone may cost you around $1,500. You do a little bit more math: that's $1,500 times two semesters per year times four years? Whew! It looks like homelessness may be in your near future, you think. How can you afford to live or have a little fun in college when every dime you may have saved up will be eaten away by books just to pass your classes? How can you afford to pursue your dreams of graduating college and getting a good-paying job to start the life you hoped to have??

Allow me to introduce myself. I am Dr. Clement Ogunyemi (better known as the Finance Doctor®). I am from the small town of Grambling, Louisiana, where I attended Grambling State University. I sat exactly where many of you are back in 2005 and thought to myself, "There has to be a better way!" I have been where you are now, and I am here to tell you that there is a way to achieve financial independence, and it is possible to start today. As you flip through this book, I want you to use this not only as motivation, but as a guide to achieve ultimate financial freedom.

The only thing I ask of you is that you return the favor: share your stories with those who come after you . . . share your journey, pitfalls, and successes with each and every person you can help through this same thing.

And know this: it won't be easy, but it will be worth it. There will be some things you may have to delay. There will be some sacrifices you will have to make. Sometimes this journey will get tough, but nothing worthwhile is easy.

Welcome to

FINANCIAL FREEDOM!

Now, before we move on to the strategies, I'd like you to fill out the following Planning Questionnaire to gain some insight into where you are now in your financial journey.

PLANNING QUESTIONNAIRE

Please answer the following questions as honestly as possible.

I feel sure about my ability to manage my own finances.

    a. Completely agree

    b. Somewhat agree

    c. Agree

    d. Somewhat disagree

    e. Disagree

    f. Completely disagree

I am interested in increasing my financial knowledge.

    a. Completely agree

    b. Somewhat agree

    c. Agree

    d. Somewhat disagree

    e. Disagree

    f. Completely disagree

If so, why?

_____

_____

_____

_____

_____

How important is spending less than your income?

    a.   Not important
    b.   Somewhat unimportant
    c.   Somewhat important
    d.   Very important

How important is having a savings/investment plan?

    a.   Not important
    b.   Somewhat unimportant
    c.   Somewhat important
    d.   Very important

How important is maintaining sufficient financial records?

    a.   Not important
    b.   Somewhat unimportant
    c.   Somewhat important
    d.   Very important

I feel in control of my financial situation.

    a.   Completely agree
    b.   Somewhat agree
    c.   Agree
    d.   Somewhat disagree
    e.   Disagree
    f.   Completely disagree

I carefully consider whether or not I can afford something *before* buying it.

    a. Completely agree
    b. Somewhat agree
    c. Agree
    d. Somewhat disagree
    e. Disagree
    f. Completely disagree

I tend to live for today and let tomorrow take care of itself.

    a. Completely agree
    b. Somewhat agree
    c. Agree
    d. Somewhat disagree
    e. Disagree
    f. Completely disagree

My finances are a significant source of worry for me.

    a. Completely agree
    b. Somewhat agree
    c. Agree
    d. Somewhat disagree
    e. Disagree
    f. Completely disagree

Each paycheck, I look back and wonder where my money went.

    a.   Completely agree

    b.   Somewhat agree

    c.   Agree

    d.   Somewhat disagree

    e.   Disagree

    f.   Completely disagree

I set long-term financial goals and strive to achieve them.

    a.   Completely agree

    b.   Somewhat agree

    c.   Agree

    d.   Somewhat disagree

    e.   Disagree

    f.   Completely disagree

Saving and investing money is important to me.

    a.   Completely agree

    b.   Somewhat agree

    c.   Agree

    d.   Somewhat disagree

    e.   Disagree

    f.   Completely disagree

I would describe my financial attitude/behavior as follows:

a. Very frugal – Not a lot of spending; saving money as much and as often as I can.
b. Somewhat frugal – Saving money often.
c. Neutral/unsure
d. Somewhat prone to spend; rarely saving money.
e. Very prone to spend; rarely, if ever, saving money.

I budget & track my spending.

a. Completely agree
b. Somewhat agree
c. Agree
d. Somewhat disagree
e. Disagree
f. Completely disagree

I have no problem using a credit card for purchases that I cannot afford/do not have the money in the bank to purchase.

a. Completely agree
b. Somewhat agree
c. Agree
d. Somewhat disagree
e. Disagree
f. Completely disagree

I pay my bills on time.

    a.   Completely agree

    b.   Somewhat agree

    c.   Agree

    d.   Somewhat disagree

    e.   Disagree

    f.   Completely disagree

I work extra hours to be able to pay my bills.

    a.   Completely agree

    b.   Somewhat agree

    c.   Agree

    d.   Somewhat disagree

    e.   Disagree

    f.   Completely disagree

I read and do research to increase my personal financial knowledge.

    a.   Completely agree

    b.   Somewhat agree

    c.   Agree

    d.   Somewhat disagree

    e.   Disagree

    f.   Completely disagree

Who did you learn your money-management skills from? (Select all that apply.)

a. Parents
b. Friends
c. School
d. Books
e. Social media
f. YouTube
g. Job
h. Life experiences
i. Financial planner/advisor

Which financial topics were discussed in your home growing up? (Select all that apply.)

a. Budgeting
b. Saving
c. Paying bills
d. Investing
e. Taxes
f. Credit
g. Interest rates
h. Transparency in finances
i. Tithing/philanthropy
j. Student loans

Growing up, how were finances handled within your household? (Select all that apply.)

a. Finance discussions usually led to arguments.
b. My family openly discussed finances.
c. My parents made it a point to discuss finances with the entire household.
d. We did not explicitly discuss finances, but my parents led by example.
e. I was included in the household's financial decision-making.

TOP 5

My Top 5 Financial Goals Are:

1. _____

2. _____

3. _____

4. _____

5. _____

Make sure your goals are realistic, attainable, and measurable.

CHAPTER 1

SOMETIMES YOU HAVE TO "SCHOOL WITHIN YOUR MEANS"

The "powers that be" have taught us to go to a "good school" . . . one with prestige and history . . . make connections, graduate, and go on to our corporate, six-figure job. You know . . . the Harvards, the Yales, UPenn, etc., etc., etc. Now, while I have heard nothing but good things about those schools, sometimes it just isn't feasible to attend. Our scholastic accolades may say yes, but our pockets say a resounding NO. What ends up happening is we get accepted to these magnificent schools, only to find out that we will graduate in extreme debt and the stress of trying to at least earn a fraction of that tuition back, by way of a six- or seven-figure salary fresh out of college. That large salary sounds good. But how realistic is it that we will make it right out of college? At the time of the publishing of this book, the average Ivy League tuition is $57K–$66K per year, or $229K–$264K over four years. And that will only go up each year! The median pay for Ivy League graduates after three years of work experience is $86K. I won't bore you any further with the statistics, but you do the math.

Allow me to tell you my Ivy League story. I was a bright-eyed, high school junior. I knew that college was the only option in my household. (My parents were very clear on this, LOL.) I applied at every single big-name school I could think of. I was so excited to tell my parents that I had applied at Yale, Harvard, Brown, UC Berkley, etc. Then the day came when I received responses from these schools. "OMGEE," I thought, "I got accepted to these schools!" I saved every single acceptance letter from these schools.

Then came the tough question, "How on earth could we (yes, we) afford to attend such expensive schools?" I applied for scholarships but quickly discovered they wouldn't even cover a fraction of my school costs, not to mention the books I would have to buy each year! Knowing that I had to go to college, I quickly had to pivot and ask myself, "Where can I go to college affordably while getting a quality education?" It was at that moment that my parents' constant lecturing came to mind. They had taught us that there were ways that you could not only go to school for free (via scholarships) but in some instances get paid to go to school. I thought, "Now they're talking my language!"

I told my parents that I was open to going to the "highest bidder," who could put me in the best position to win once I graduated. I knew I did not want to spend the first ten to fifteen years of my working life to paying back student loans. So, what did I do? I started looking at schools that offered full-ride scholarships. Then I applied to these schools' scholarships as well as external scholarships. It was such a gratifying feeling to get those letters telling me that not only had I been accepted, but I was not going to be a financial burden to my parents, nor would I have to accumulate a mountain of student loan debt. I could go get a quality education and get paid to do so.

During my collegiate tenure, I was in the same rooms and competing for the same jobs and internships as my Ivy League peers. I was applying for and being awarded the same scholarships that my Ivy League peers were applying for. I was able to compete and in many instances win, when placed side by side with my peers attending more prestigious institutions.

Please do not misconstrue my message here. Yes, an Ivy League education looks great on a resume. However, you can get a quality education from other, less expensive schools as well. You do not have to graduate with a mountain of debt and a bleak financial future. You can start your adult life with forward financial momentum. Luckily for you, I am here to provide you with a blueprint to win, and win big. If you are reading this book, then you have taken a huge step, and I am beyond proud of you. You will be more than just a student loan statistic. I hope that many more students follow your lead and get just as much out of this book and their college experience as you do.

KEY TAKEAWAYS

1. Ivy League schools are not always the way to go.
2. Sometimes you need to look at schools that are solid schools with a reputable program in your desired area(s) of study.

QUESTIONS FOR REFLECTION

1. What are your dream schools?
2. How would you feel if you were unable to attend one of your dream schools?

CHAPTER 2

TAKING THE ALTERNATE ROUTE TO YOUR DREAM SCHOOL

JUNIOR COLLEGE & COMMUNITY COLLEGE

THE ROAD NOT TAKEN

Two roads diverged in a yellow wood,
And sorry I could not travel both
And be one traveler, long I stood
And looked down one as far as I could

To where it bent in the undergrowth;
Then took the other, as just as fair,
And having perhaps the better claim,
Because it was grassy and wanted wear

Though as for the passing there
Had worn them both the same,
And both that morning equally lay
In leaves no step had trodden black.

Oh, I kept the first for another day!
Yet knowing how way leads onto way,
I doubted if I should ever come back.
I shall be telling this with a sigh

Somewhere ages and ages hence;
Two roads diverged in a wood, and I—
I took the one less traveled by,
And that has made all the difference.

—*Robert Frost (1916)*

So, you didn't get any scholarships to attend your "dream school" fresh out of high school. Are what are you going to do? Cry about it? Skip college? Take out enough student loans to last you a lifetime? While I will not judge you for any of the aforementioned, I will provide you with an alternative—junior college or community college. Both of these options are much more affordable and allow you time to (for lack of a better term) prove yourself. Going to a junior or community college gives you time to improve your grades, community service, etc. and get on your dream school's radar. It also allows you to knock out your core classes at a much lower cost to you. One thing I will warn here is to make sure these course credits will count toward the degree program you intend to pursue. Taking this route also gives you time to work and save up some money while completing your first two years of college! If that doesn't halfway excite you, then you don't have a pulse. If you don't believe me, let's look at some numbers.

As of the publishing of this book, the average annual cost to attend a community college within your home state is roughly $5,155 per year and $8,835 per year for out-of-state students. Where does this fall in relation to the average cost of a four-year degree? Well, the average cost of attending a four-year college in the United States is roughly $25,000 per year. That's right, it is roughly four to five times more expensive! So tell me, does it make sense to knock out your first two years of college at a much lower cost? I most certainly would!

CONSIDER LIVING WITH YOUR PARENTS (JUST A LITTLE LONGER)

I just *know* you didn't want to hear that! However, think *group economics*! Let me give you my story on this real quick. Growing up, everyone around us believed that you were grown grown when you turned eighteen and you should move out and "be an adult." In fact, most parents would live by, "I can't wait until these kids are eighteen so they can get out of my house!" Now, while I don't fault parents for simply doing what they had been taught, I want us all to realize how quickly this could set our kids up for failure!

Naturally, I always said that as soon as I turned eighteen, I was moving out to "be my own man." That was just what we all thought you did. Little did I know that was not in the cards. I moved "away" for college to attend the University of New Orleans—far away enough from home but still close (just in case I needed my mommy). Well, in 2005, I was in school at UNO for one week . . . yes, just one week, before Hurricane Katrina ravaged our state. So I was forced to go back home, without a return date in site, amongst the devastation. I initially planned to sit out the semester and wait until UNO reopened. However, my mother suggested I go to Grambling (at home) so I did not lose any time at school. Since I was, in essence, starting over, I did remain in my parents' house, got a job, and attended classes at Grambling. Although I was working and offered to pay some bills, my parents refused my money. I was immediately offended. How could they not allow this "grown man" who was living in their house to pay some bills like a "real adult"? It wasn't until I was an adult that I realized what my parents had truly done. They gave me an economic boost so I could leave the nest (when the time was right) comfortably. I moved out my senior year of college and bought a house! Yes, at the age of twenty-one, I bought my first house. Was I nervous? Absolutely! Scared? Most definitely! My parents allowed me to stay home and begin accumulating wealth and assets while in college, which jumpstarted my current financial freedom journey. They went against the "norm" of kicking your baby bird out of the nest without the requisite tools to fend for themselves in this wild world.

This is what I mean by group economics! Group economics has been around for centuries. Its foundations lie in recognizing the power of unity and the leveraging of shared resources in order to achieve an economic goal. Group economics is when a group of people pool their resources (historically money), skills, knowledge, and networks together to reach a common goal that may not have been reached on their own. By harnessing their collective power, communities can conquer common challenges, such as limited access to capital, economic disparities, and limited market opportunities. One of the most well-known and basic forms of group economics is a family of ten living in one house. Everyone contributes to the economics of that household. When one person is ready to move on, *everyone* chips in! They pool their money together to accomplish the goals of every single individual within their "economy." What ends up happening is that everyone can leave the "group" economically stable and with some assets to begin their own new group economics. Brilliant, right? For some, group economics looks like having roommates during and after college. For others, it looks like staying home with your parents for a little while longer before spreading your wings to soar solo like an eagle.

KEY TAKEAWAYS

1. Big colleges aren't the only option. Consider knocking out your core classes at a junior college or community college.
2. Living with your parents a little longer to save money may not be such a bad idea. (Think group economics.)

QUESTIONS FOR REFLECTION

1. How many times has the cost of attending college made you feel discouraged?
2. What are some ways you can save money the first couple years of your college career?
3. Has the increasing cost of attending college made you feel anxious about your future?

CHAPTER 3

FINDING MONEY . . . MONEY FINDING ME

*College should not be a **debt sentence**. You should not walk across that stage feeling anxious and crushed by mounds of debt that are nearly impossible to ever payoff!*

'm not sure if anyone has told you, but it costs very real money to attend college. That degree most certainly is not free . . . but it *can* be. Yes, going to school to get a good education (with the idea of eventually getting a good job) is not a cheap endeavor. However, do not let that paralyze you with fear. Use it as motivation . . . motivation to get creative and find money to realize your dreams, your hopes, your aspirations. In this chapter, I will walk you through several different funding sources that can alleviate the stress of having to pay for college. And here's a little secret: you don't have to be limited to one of these strategies. In fact, I encourage you to use several in tandem. Find a strategy (or strategies) that fit your situation and that make sense for you. Make your plan **written** and **attainable**.

FIRST THINGS FIRST - THE FAFSA

The Free Application for Federal Student Aid, or FAFSA, is a form completed by students each year to determine their eligibility for financial assistance/aid. Yes, it is free to apply. So, why not fill it out ASAP? The FAFSA will determine if you are eligible to receive any of the absolutely free money that your school of choice or governments are handing out to students all around you. I know you're probably wondering who does not have to fill out the FAFSA each year, and I've got the answer to your inquiring minds. If (and only if) you can afford to pay cash for college, then you don't need to fill out a FAFSA. However, if this is not you, fill that FAFSA out every year that you plan to attend college.

Now, what information is collected on the FAFSA? When filling out your FAFSA, you will need to provide your demographic and financial information (via tax returns) and, in most cases, the same information for your parents. When filling out your FAFSA, you will also be given the option to have your FAFSA data sent to up to ten schools of your choice. The financial information you provide helps colleges determine your ability to pay for school and how much aid you truly need to help you afford school. In other words, you have to have a FAFSA on file to be able to apply for federal student aid, work-study programs, state aid, school-sponsored aid, grants, and, if push comes to shove, student loans. **A good rule of thumb for high schoolers is to always fill out the FAFSA, even if you decide not to go to college.**

Now that we've gotten the "legal stuff" out of the way, let's get into the fun stuff. Where on earth do we find all this free money to go to school? I am so glad you asked. Let's talk through several different ways you can go to school. Note: The following section is for students who don't happen to have six figures set aside to pay cash for college. LOL. Really, the next sections are for **every single student considering going to college**.

SCHOLARSHIP

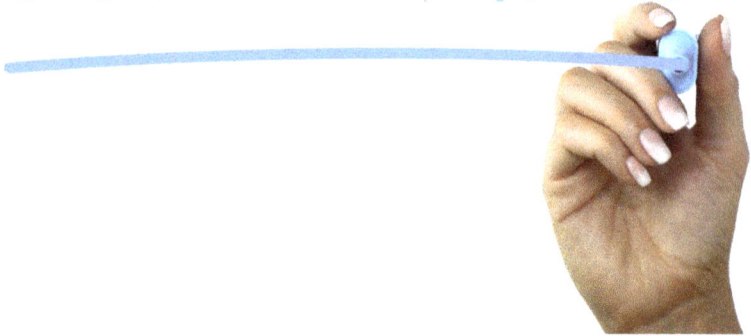

WHAT IS A SCHOLARSHIP?

A scholarship is a form of financial assistance/aid awarded to a student to pursue higher education. Scholarships are typically based on either academic achievement or other preset criteria, such as community service or merit. These criteria are usually set by the person or entity giving that scholarship. Scholarships can be a one-time payment or renewable each semester or year. The funds from scholarships can either be disbursed directly to you, the student, or to the school you are attending, to cover your expenses. The two most common types of scholarships are need-based and merit-based. Merit-based scholarships are awarded based on criteria related to your academic and/or extra-curricular achievements, such as high test scores, community service, or high grades. Conversely, need-based scholarships are awarded to you when it has been determined that you may not have the financial means to pay for college independently. Now do you see why the FAFSA is so important?

Scholarships come from various sources and come in all shapes and sizes. The four different scholarship types are as follows:

- **Federal:** These will almost always be need-based. Pell grants (which will discuss later) are the biggest federal grant.
- **State:** A good place to start your search for State financial aid is the National Association of Student Financial Aid Administration (NASFAA). You can search for scholarships specific to your state.
- **School-specific scholarships:** When you apply to your school, they will typically either (a) award you a merit-based scholarship or (b) have you fill out a separate application for scholarships at that specific school.
- **Private scholarships:** These scholarships are awarded by companies (like Walmart and Nike), foundations, non-profits, religious groups, and professional organizations. Most of these awards are smaller one-time awards.

The biggest thing to remember about scholarships is that you do not have to repay them! That's right, the money truly is free and truly does help you pay for college!

WHO CAN APPLY FOR SCHOLARSHIPS?

Literally anyone can apply! So why not just do it (like Nike)? Please understand (and read this very carefully), you may not get every scholarship that you apply for. However, do not ever let that discourage you. In fact, use that as motivation to get the next one. If a member of the scholarship committee reaches out to you to tell you that they "went another direction," ask them, "What could I do to make my applications more marketable?" A scholarship board should want to see you succeed and should have no issue helping you reach success at the next level (emphasis on should). I am not sure how many math and statistics experts are reading this, but the more scholarships you apply to, the more opportunities you have to win and the higher the likelihood that you will be awarded a scholarship or two along the way. So, apply your little heart out, and do not be discouraged. My recommendation is to spend one hour every day applying for scholarships. Surely you can spare one hour of your time to get some free money, right?

WHERE CAN I FIND SCHOLARSHIPS?

I know you are thinking, "Geez, this seems like a lot of work. If only there were websites and databases where I could go to find and apply for multiple scholarships." Good thing I am here to help. There are several different websites you can use to search for thousands of scholarships, a lot like applying for a job. Here are a few resources that I have found and/or used to find and apply for scholarships:

Scholly – www.myscholly.com
Fastweb – www.fastweb.com
Going Merry - www.goingmerry.com
Scholarships.com – www.scholarships.com
BigFuture – https://bigfuture.collegeboard.org/pay-for-college/scholarship-directory

APPLYING FOR SCHOLARSHIPS

Now that you know *where* to search for scholarships, I am sure you are wondering *how* to apply for these scholarships once you find them. When applying for scholarships, I cannot stress enough how important it is to know the deadlines. The absolute worst feeling in the world is knowing that you want to apply for a scholarship, but you put it off, only to discover later that you have missed the deadline and, thus, missed out on the free money you could have been in line for. Here's another tidbit of information that may get the juices flowing: it is free to apply for most scholarships! The only cost to you is your time. I don't know about you, but I am willing to sacrifice a little of my time in order to "secure the bag."

PREPARING A SCHOLARSHIP-WINNING ESSAY

Most scholarships (especially the larger dollar amounts) will require you to write an essay. The essay may be one of the most important aspects in the pursuit of winning a scholarship. With all things being equal between so many candidates, the essay may be the one piece that gives you the edge and the final nod on being awarded that coveted scholarship. Make sure you write an essay that stands out from the rest.

How do you do that? First, begin your essay with a *wow statement* that will grab the attention of your reader *immediately*. Realize that the committee probably reads hundreds or thousands of essays by the time they get to yours. The last thing you want to do is bore them to death or have a cookie-cutter essay that sounds just like the rest. Next, do *not* make the mistake of restating the essay question or prompt in your opening sentence. Assume that the committee already knows the question and prompt (which is a very valid assumption). And finally, remember that you want to engage your reader. One way is to force the reader to see what you see, feel what you feel, hear what you hear . . . Here is an example essay question that is pretty common:

Tell me about a time when you faced adversity.
Be sure to discuss how you overcame and
achieved your desired outcome.

Now, you may be tempted to begin your response with:

I faced adversity when . . . and overcame it by . . .

While this response is probably the most direct answer to the question, it is rather boring and may put your reader to sleep. Instead, pull the reader into *your* life to see things through *your* eyes. Maybe consider beginning your essay like this:

It was a cold Tuesday morning, in the small town of Grambling, LA. As I gazed out my window, I wondered how I would find the will to roll out of my bed . . .

With an intro like this, you immediately pull the reader in to feel what you felt, to see what you saw, and to ultimately take that journey with you. Create a "sense of wonder" that will make the reader want to learn more about you.

I cannot stress enough how important it is to **read the essay criteria**. My family provides a scholarship every year. It surprises me when students get disqualified for not following one of the essay criteria, such as the word count. Most programs, like Microsoft Word, tell you exactly how many words are in your writings. Don't let a small technicality disqualify you from getting a scholarship that you would otherwise get. Simply put, pay attention to the details.

The following is a pretty standard rubric that scholarship committees use when evaluating your essays:

Focus/Main Point	The essay is focused, purposeful, and reflects original insight and ideas.
Support	Persuasively supports main point with well-developed reasons and/or examples.
Organization & Format	Effectively organizes ideas to build logical, coherent argument.
Language Use & Style	Effective and creative use of elements of style to enhance meaning.
Conventions	Uses correct grammar, spelling, and punctuation throughout, with very few errors.

Also, a little secret I learned during my time applying for scholarships that I tell the students I help apply for scholarships is this: keep your essays! Why? Because many of the scholarship essay questions are very similar. You can use the same essay (sometimes with some minor tweaks) to apply for multiple scholarships.

When writing your essays, do not hesitate to reach out for help from an English teacher or other writer who doesn't mind looking it over for you. Also, consider using software add-ons, such as Grammarly, to assist in your writing.

The following is a scholarship essay that Ana wrote when applying for and _won_ the $39,500 New York University College of Arts and Science scholarship. The question was:

Explain something that made a big impact in your life.

"If you can't live off of it, it is useless." My parents were talking about ice skating: my passion. I started skating as a ten-year-old in Spain, admiring how difficulty and grace intertwine to create beautiful programs, but no one imagined I would still be on the ice seven years and one country later. Even more unimaginable was the thought that ice skating might become one of the most useful parts of my life.

I was born in Mexico to two Spanish speakers; thus, Spanish was my first language. We then moved to Spain when I was six, before finally arriving in California around my thirteenth birthday. Each change introduced countless challenges, but the hardest part of moving to America, for me, was learning English. Laminated index cards, color-coded and full of vocabulary, became part of my daily life. As someone who loves to engage in a conversation, it was very hard to feel as if my tongue was cut off. Only at the ice rink could I be myself; the feeling of the cold rink breeze embracing me, the ripping sound of blades touching the ice, even the occasional ice burning my skin as I fell—these were my few constants. I did not need to worry about mispronouncing "axel" as "aksal." Rather, I just needed to glide and deliver the jump.

From its good-natured bruise-counting competitions to its culture of hard work and perseverance, ice skating provided the nurturing environment that made my other challenges worthwhile. Knowing that each moment on the ice represented a financial sacrifice for my family, I cherished every second I got. Often this meant waking up every morning at 4 a.m. to practice what I had learned in my few precious minutes of coaching. It meant assisting in group lessons to earn extra skating time and taking my conditioning off ice by joining my high school varsity running teams. Even as I began to make friends and lose my fear of speaking, the rink was my sanctuary. Eventually, however, the only way to keep improving was to pay for more coaching, which my family could not afford. And so I started tutoring Spanish.

Now, the biggest passion of my life is supported by my most natural ability. I have had over thirty Spanish students, ranging in age from three to forty and spanning many ethnic backgrounds. I currently work with fifteen students each week, each with different needs and ways of learning. Drawing on my own experiences as both a second-language learner and a figure skater, I assign personal, interactive exercises, make jokes to keep my students' mindset positive, and never give away the right answers. When I first started learning my axel jump, my coach told me I would have to fall at least five hundred times (about a year of falls!) in order to land it. Likewise, I have my students embrace every detail of a mistake until they can begin to recognize new errors when they see them. I encourage them to expand their horizons and take pride in preparing them for new interactions and opportunities.

Although I agree that I will never live off of ice skating, the education and skills I have gained from it have opened countless doors. Ice skating has given me the resilience, work ethic, and inspiration to develop as a teacher and an English speaker. It has improved my academic performance by teaching me rhythm, health, and routine. It also reminds me that a passion does not have to produce money in order for it to hold immense value. Ceramics, for instance, challenges me to experiment with the messy and unexpected, while painting reminds me to be adventurous and patient with my forms of self-expression. I don't know yet what I will live off of from day to day as I mature; however, the skills my passions have provided me are life-long and irreplaceable.

NEVER STOP APPLYING

The scholarship journey doesn't end once you get to college. Apply for new scholarships every year. There are scholarships based on your college classification (freshman, sophomore, junior, senior). If your grades weren't where you wanted them to be when you graduated high school but they have now improved, apply for scholarships. I definitely applied for new scholarships every year. The biggest scholarship I received was during the summer going into my junior year. I secured a $10,000 scholarship from Morgan Stanley, which I was able to use in addition to the scholarships I already had! I was already going to school for free and receiving a small refund, so the new $10K was money I could put directly into my pockets! Now imagine *that* as a college student.

Always remember that the scholarships that are renewable annually must be maintained. So please don't slack off and lose funding. I have seen it happen. Understand the requirements for keeping those scholarships. Some requirements may be related to maintaining a specific GPA. Other criteria may involve maintaining a certain number of credit hours per year or may be tied to a specific college major.

One last tidbit of information on scholarships: Some states offer scholarships for you to stay in the state you are a resident of! Let's take Louisiana, for example. Louisiana offers the TOPS (Taylor Opportunity Program for Students) scholarship to Louisiana residents who attend a Louisiana public college or university, Louisiana approved proprietary and cosmetology schools, or institutions that are a part of the Louisiana Association of Independent Colleges & Universities. At the time of the publication of this book, for students to be eligible to receive TOPS, they had to maintain a minimum cumulative GPA through high school, score a minimum of a 23 on the ACT, and complete at least 19 Core units of the TOPS Core Curriculum. You must also enroll full time as a first-time freshman by the first semester following the first anniversary of high school graduation. TOPS has historically paid a large portion of tuition at the institution types listed above *plus* an annual stipend (meaning money directly to you!). You can visit the TOPS website to see exactly which TOPS award you qualify for and how much each award pays to Louisiana residents. Make sure to check the various opportunities and requirements for your state, should you choose to remain in your home state to attend college.

AN EXERCISE TO HELP YOU SEARCH FOR SCHOLARSHIPS

There are literally scholarships for *everything*. Literally, all you have to do is look. I am here to help you begin your search process. Below is an exercise to get the wheels turning and help you find all the free money out there.

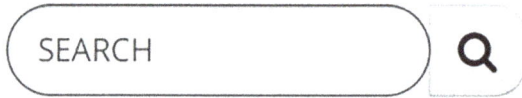

What am I passionate about?

What brings me joy?

What circumstances have I been through in my life?

What is my social and economic background?

What are my favorite products/companies?

What are my hobbies?

When you complete the questions above, pull up a web browser and search for scholarships related to the items you listed. For example, if your social/economic background answer is that you come from a single-parent home, then Google "children of single parents scholarships." If your favorite company is Nike, then search for "Nike scholarships."

Bonus: The next time you are walking through your local neighborhood Walmart or other grocer, look on the shelf (yes, any shelf works). See who manufacturers the products on that shelf: (for example, Coke, Pepsi, Kraft, Tyson, etc.). Go to Google, type in the company name, put the word "scholarship" behind it, and click Enter. You can even see if the store you are walking through has any scholarship opportunities. You can repeat this small exercise with the shoes you are wearing, the handbag you are carrying, or even the computer or cell phone you are currently using. Alternatively, search online for a list of brands that offer scholarships. You're welcome, LOL.

MY SCHOLARSHIP STORY

Now I'd like to tell you *my* scholarship story. When I was in high school, there were two things I knew for a fact: (1) My parents required us to go to college, and (2) I was not going to pay for school (since my parents forced me to go (LOL). Knowing these two facts, it was my mission to get this right. So what did I do? I made sure my grades were tight. I filled out that darned FAFSA, and I started applying for every scholarship under the sun. I applied for Coke scholarships, Walmart scholarships, Nike scholarships . . . I even applied for scholarships I did not likely qualify for. I honestly did not care about the criteria. I was on fire and was not going to leave any money on the table. I applied for Latino scholarships (knowing I am 100% Black) with the mindset that if they did not receive enough qualified Latino applicants, then guess who was next in line. There were several times that the scholarship committee had to reconsider their criteria and because I wasn't afraid to apply, and I was able to take advantage of that scholarship opportunity. Just like Wayne Gretzky once said, "You miss 100% of the shots you don't take."

And the scholarship applications didn't stop just because I started college. I applied for new scholarships every year. There were times when I was competing against students from Princeton, Harvard, and Yale . . . and winning. My biggest scholarship came from Morgan Stanley. Like I told you earlier I applied, competed, and was awarded a $10,000 scholarship that went straight into my pockets. My senior year of college, I had enough scholarship money that I not only went to school for free, but I was making money to be a student. Why? Because I wasn't afraid to apply . . . I wasn't afraid of being told no, and even when I was told no, I would apply for that scholarship plus more the following year. It became a very fun (and profitable) game for me—a game that jumpstarted my entire financial future and set me up for success during school and after graduation. I tell you my story not to brag, but to tell you to apply . . . to not be afraid of being told no . . . because there is plenty of money out there, just waiting for you.

PELL GRANTS

Pell grants are a form of need-based financial aid awarded by the US Department of Education. These grants are awarded to low-income students to help supplement the costs of going to college (such as books, housing, tuition and fees, etc.). To begin qualifying for Pell Grants, you will have to have a FAFSA on file, which is used to determine your expected family contribution (EFC). Pell grants do not have to be repaid. However, make sure you read the stipulations carefully, as some can be taken away if your enrollment status changes after the funds have been disbursed. The good thing about Pell Grants is that you can still apply for other financial aid. Again, it is free money, so long as you do your part (pursue your degree, maintain enrollment, maintain a solid GPA). One limit of Pell Grants is the lifetime eligibility, or the total amount of Pell Grant money you can receive. As of the publication of this book, that limit is six years or twelve semesters.

WORK-STUDY PROGRAMS

Federal work-study programs are part-time jobs for undergraduate and graduate students who have demonstrated a financial need. The work-study program allows you to earn money that can be used to help pay for your educational expenses. Work-study programs typically promote community service and encourage you to conduct work related to your course of study. Work-study programs are available to you whether you are a full-time or part-time student. In order to enroll in a work-study, your school must participate in the Federal Work-Study Program. You should always check with financial aid to better understand if your school is a participating institution. You will earn at least the federal minimum wage at the time of your work-study. The total you earn cannot exceed the amount of the Federal Work-Study Award. One of the benefits of doing a work-study, as opposed to a regular job, is the fact that the employer will do their best to work around your school schedule and take into consideration your class hours and workload.

FEDERAL WORK-STUDY QUICK FACTS

- Provides part-time work while you're enrolled in school.
- Available to undergraduate and graduate students (full- or part-time students).
- Students must have demonstrated a financial need.
- Your school must be a participant in the Federal Work-Study Program. (Check with the school's financial aid office).

- Offers flexibility – Your work hours will operate around your school schedule, course load, etc.
- You will earn at least the federal minimum wage, sometimes more, depending on the job.

INTERNSHIPS (DO NOT MISS OUT)

An internship is a professional learning experience that integrates knowledge and theory learned in the classroom with practical applications and skills development in a professional environment. Ideally, an internship provides you with the opportunity to work on relevant projects, learn about your field, make industry connections, and develop hard and soft skills. Internships can be paid or unpaid.

I was fortunate to have only received paid internships, which provided both experience and some extra money in my pockets. Now, while there are many paid internships out there, hear me and hear me good: **Do not miss out on a great experience that could change the entire trajectory of your adult life just because the pay isn't what you think it should be.** For example, let's imagine that your dream employer comes to you and asks you to participate in their summer internship program. However, the pay isn't where you think it should be or the internship is unpaid. First, I would try to negotiate. If they are firm, then don't fret. Go to a website like Glassdoor.com and look at what an entry-level position at that company pays. Then ask yourself how much that free internship is truly worth, especially if it has the potential to lead to a full-time good-paying job after you graduate. Sometimes you have to be comfortable being uncomfortable for a short season. My internship experience was a huge blessing, since it was paid *and* offered me the job I truly wanted after graduation, with a really nice salary. The only thing that derailed that plan was the market crash of 2008. Otherwise, I made sure to put my best foot forward during that internship and stayed in contact with the hiring team up until I graduated.

Oftentimes, when you graduate and go to apply for your first job, you are met with the infamous, "You don't have enough experience for this job." I cannot tell you how many times I heard that, and I always wondered, "Well how on earth am I supposed to gain experience when no one will give me that experience?" Well, let me tell you: internships are a way to combat that little statement employers like to say to you.

I am often asked if I recommend students doing internships. And the answer is absolutely: do them early and often. Yes, your summers are for having fun, but make sure you are strategic and are still maximizing those summers by gaining experience. Here's a little secret: No one said that the two cannot coincide! I always applied for internships in places I wanted to visit or places I enjoyed going, like Florida, New York, California, etc. Now, I didn't always get internships in those places, but that didn't stop me from trying. So, yes, each and every student should search for and apply for internships in their field of study.

Sometimes an internship will help you discover that you may not enjoy your major as much as you thought—and I am speaking from personal experience here. I began my college career in forensic chemistry. I watched (and still do watch) all the crime shows and just knew I was the missing piece to finding every killer out there by looking underneath a microscope for that tiny trace evidence. Well, I had an internship that made me completely pivot. I can recall being in a super-cold lab for eight to ten hours a day, sometimes waiting all day for lab results, which felt comparable to watching paint dry. One day as I sat alone in a freezing-cold lab in New Orleans, Louisiana, I wondered if this was something I could see myself doing for the next fifteen to twenty years. The answer was no! I switched my major to business that summer and never looked back.

Don't get me wrong, I still love forensics and watch my shows every night, and maybe one day I will go back and get that degree just because, but for now, I think I made the right decision. The moral of that story is that internships can be valuable in a number of ways. You can get paid (or not) while gaining valuable experience and getting a picture of the type of work you may be doing in your major field after graduation. So, intern as early as you can, learn about your potential profession, and structure your learning career and decision-making around that.

EMPLOYER TUITION ASSISTANCE & REIMBURSEMENT

Sometimes, when you enter college, you already have a job, which can be extremely advantageous, if you leverage that relationship correctly. Many times, we lack knowledge simply because we don't ask the right questions or know the right questions to ask. When an employer is paying you as their employee, they are invested in you. And when that employer can see the benefit of you gaining knowledge and skills to make them more profitable, then of course they are more inclined to help you get there. One thing to be aware of, though, is this: many times, if an employer pays for any portion of your education or certifications, they may have you sign a contract that requires you to stay with them for a certain amount of time after you finish the program, or you have to repay them. Like I said, they want a return on that investment and want you to impact their bottom line.

Studies have shown that for every $1 a company spends on educational assistance programs, they save an average of $1.29 in recruitment costs. Additionally, the increased employee development gives companies more promotable staff, thus reducing the costs of recruiting, hiring, and training new personnel. For example, I worked for Walgreens while I was in college. Walgreens was growing rapidly at the time and always looking for new store managers and assistant managers. What better place to find them than right within their organization! So naturally, because I was there learning the inner workings of the organization and a business major, this was a natural marriage. They were very willing to invest in me, with the idea that I would be a good store manager for them after graduation. I only knew about these opportunities because I was always asking questions and wanting to understand how we could foster a mutually beneficial relationship during my time there. Another really solid company that currently offers tuition assistance and/or reimbursement is Walmart, no matter what level you are currently at (cashier, customer service, warehouse, cart pusher, etc.). Just ask! Always remember that Walmart does have a corporate office and store manager positions. With that in mind, understand that your current job is just a means to an end.

SO, WHAT EXACTLY IS TUITION ASSISTANCE/REIMBURSEMENT?

Tuition reimbursement is an employee benefit where the employer pays for a pre-determined amount of continuing education credits or college coursework to be applied toward a degree. These programs are designed to help employees (who want to) advance their education as it relates to their current career track by increasing their industry knowledge and developing advanced skills. One statistic I found alarming while writing this book is that only 2% of eligible employees take advantage of tuition reimbursement/assistance programs, while at least 60% of working professionals don't even know that these benefits are available. Make sure you understand the reimbursement and assistance policies and ask questions. Most times, the eligible coursework has to be related to your current job. Your employer may also require you to maintain certain grades.

The United States Military also offers education assistance programs to its members and their families. Please make sure you understand the stipulations and requirements of utilizing their education assistance programs before signing up for them. They have very specific criteria and time commitments that must be met, or you may be required to repay the money (which would definitely suck).

A SECTION FOR PARENTS (529 PLANS)

So far in this book, I've focused a lot of my attention on the students getting ready to go to college. However, I want to take a moment to appreciate the parents who have guided them to this point. I would also like to provide a good blueprint for helping your students set aside money to offset some of the rising costs of attending school. One method (which is also beneficial to you, parents) is the state's 529 plans. Now, before we continue, understand that these plans are state-specific so please check with your state before signing up. A 529 plan (Also known as a qualified tuition program) is a state-sponsored investment account that allows you to save money for education expenses. The 529 plan can offer you tax benefits, including tax-deferred earnings and tax-free withdrawals for **qualified education expenses**. Qualified expenses include tuition, room and board, books, supplies, and other fees required by the school. Please note: Money withdrawn for nonqualified expenses is subject to a penalty plus ordinary income taxes. If your state offers 529 plans, make sure you consult your tax accountant for guidance when opening and funding the account(s). States that participate typically offer a reduction of your state taxes when you contribute to the plan.

Other types of college funding accounts include the Coverdell Education Savings Account (ESA) and the Uniform Gifts to Minors Act (UGMA) or Uniform Transfer to Minors Act (UTMA). Make sure you consult a financial adviser and your tax professional when considering opening these accounts. The earlier you start, the better. And please understand that it is *never* too late or too early to start the process.

KEY TAKEAWAYS

1. First things first – Fill out your FAFSA (**Free** Application for Federal Student Aid).
2. Scholarships can help offset the costs of going to college.
3. **Every** student should apply for scholarships.
4. Scholarships do not have to be repaid.
5. Students should apply for scholarships every year of college.
6. Most scholarships require an essay. Make sure you don't just answer the question, but tell a story that will make your essay stand out from the rest.
7. Make sure you read all the scholarship requirements **thoroughly** before submitting.
8. Get creative in your scholarship search. Think about the things you are passionate about, the things that bring you joy, your socioeconomic background, the things you have endured in life, your hobbies, your favorite products/companies, and the list goes on!
9. Other forms of financial aid include Pell grants, work studies, internships, and employer tuition assistance and reimbursement programs.

QUESTIONS FOR REFLECTION

1. How would you feel if you received enough money to go to school for free?
2. Have you started looking into scholarships for school?
3. Parents, how would you feel knowing that you helped jumpstart your child's financial future?

CHAPTER 4

"BUT I GET A FREE PIZZA"

AVOIDING THE CONSUMER DEBT TRAP

remember it like it was yesterday: I was in college and got a call to come get a free pizza! As many of you may know (or soon learn), when you are in college, you probably don't have an unlimited supply of money. So, as college students, anything free is a yes in our books! I sped down to the pizza restaurant to make sure they did not run out, only to find a looong line of my friends and classmates waiting to get their free large pizzas. As we approached, we were all greeted by some very friendly adults who handed us a few pieces of paper and informed us that in order to get our free pizza, we had to apply for a new credit card. Not thinking twice, we all remained in line and filled out those applications (no questions asked) and proceeded to get our fresh, delicious large pizzas. What a great day! The entire crew got to eat for free. But how free was this pizza, truly?

A few weeks went by, and my parents received an envelope addressed to me with a brand-new, shiny credit card inside. "Oh gosh," I thought. I knew absolutely nothing about credit or how it worked, or this new credit card I had received. I couldn't throw it away, right? I was "obligated" to use it, right? Being a young, somewhat broke college student, I used that card anytime I did not have the cash available to buy something I wanted. Before long, I realized the stupid large pizza I had received was now costing me 29% in compound interest! I blamed my friends who called me about this stupid pizza . . . I blamed the credit card companies for taking advantage of us "poor college kids." What I had to realize is that it was my fault and no one else's. I failed to do my research and thoroughly understand what I was getting myself into—and I gave them all my personal information.

Why do I tell you this story? I am glad that you asked. In college, please do not be reckless when it comes to your credit and personal information. Trust me when I say that the $10 large pizza is not worth the mounds of interest you will have to repay. There is a reason they are willing to line up hundreds of students and give them large pizzas all day—think about it. A wise man once said that everything that glitters isn't gold. Just be careful and do your research.

Most times, as a college student, you do not make enough money to maintain a credit card anyway. Small choices that you make today can have huge implications on your future financial well-being. Your future self will thank you for spending your money wisely and making good financial decisions, knowing that a free pizza isn't worth going into debt that you cannot afford to repay for years. I wish I'd had this book to guide me a little better in college, but you do, and when we know better, we do better.

The three questions I always challenge people (and myself) with before making a purchase are as follows:

1. Can I afford it?
2. Do I need it?
3. How will this purchase affect me?
   Many times, these simple questions are enough to get you out of that "free pizza" line: a small decision that could have a butterfly effect throughout the rest of your life.

KEY TAKEAWAYS

1. Getting a free pizza is not worth a credit card that you may not be able to afford.
2. Don't get caught up in the "clever" marketing.
3. Before making a purchase (especially with a credit card), ask yourself the following:
   - ☐ Can I afford it?
   - ☐ Do I truly need it?
   - ☐ How will this purchase affect me?

QUESTIONS FOR REFLECTION

1. Why do you think credit card companies target "broke" college kids?
2. When do you think is a good time to get a credit card?
3. Why do some people use credit cards for purchases, rather than saving and budgeting for those purchases?

CHAPTER 5

A CHAPTER FOR MY NIL ATHLETES

J ust in case you have been living underneath a rock over the last few years, let me tell you about this new phenomenon known as NIL. Historically, college athletes have been prohibited from receiving payment and monetizing their names, images, and likenesses. College players were required to maintain their amateur status and not allowed to play for pay. Student athletes were only allowed to receive scholarships.

So, what is NIL? NIL stands for **N**ame, **I**mage, and **L**ikeness. In essence, NIL deals allow student-athletes to be compensated for promoting, partnering with, or representing brands. Many brands find a mutually beneficial relationship with athletes, using the athletes' fame to grow their businesses. Athletes are allowed to make money through activities such as follows:

- Guest appearances and autograph signings
- Sports events
- Exhibitions
- Sponsorships
- Endorsements
- Content creation/being a social media influencer
- NFTs
- Gifts & Giveaways

WHAT NIL MEANS TO AN ATHLETE'S FINANCES

We all know that the moment we make *any* type of money, the IRS will want their cut. What this means is that while student-athletes have newfound revenue streams (some of which reach more than seven figures!), the tax implications can have a nasty sting for these athletes. But do not fear, your resident tax expert is here to provide some guidance. Please understand that tax laws change each year, and you should always consult a tax expert to ensure you are up to speed on any new guidance that comes down from the IRS. And here's the fun part: At the time of this book, they are still working out the kinks, and IRS laws are always changing (sometimes mid-year). So, here are a few tips as you begin to earn (sometimes) larger sums of money than you've ever seen:

- The money you earn *is* taxable. You will have to pay taxes on earned income.

- Make sure you report **all** the money that you earn. Now isn't the time to omit any of the payments you receive. Nine times out of ten, the IRS *will* find out.
- Most NIL athletes are considered independent contractors and may need to make quarterly estimated taxes. As an independent contractor, the company giving you the NIL should require you to fill out a W9 (which gives them important information needed to legally pay you). Be sure to find a tax pro you can trust and talk to throughout the year.
- Make sure you have an attorney who can interpret the federal, state, and local NIL laws so you can avoid any type of future litigation, disqualification, etc.
- There *is* hope, as there are certain deductions and expenses related to your name, image, and likeness that you can deduct to offset your taxable income. We will discuss several below.

If you are considered an independent contractor, you will report your income (at the end of the year) on Schedule C (profit or loss from business).

TAX BREAKS & DEDUCTIONS FOR NIL ATHLETES

I SUGGEST HAVING AN LLC SETUP & HAVING NIL PAYMENTS MADE OUT TO YOUR LLC. CONSULT A LAWYER TO MAKE SURE THE LLC IS SET UP CORRECTLY & THAT YOU HAVE THE PROPER PROTECTIONS.

Tax breaks/deductions are expenses that help you reduce taxable income, and trust me, you want to reduce what the Feds will want you to pay. So how do you know what you can deduct versus what may get you into some trouble? Well, the IRS says that you may deduct expenses that are "ordinary and necessary expenses" that you incur while operating your "trade or business."

To be engaged in a "trade or business," you must be involved in the activity with continuity and regularity and the primary purpose of the activity must be for income or profit.

Below, I have provided a list of potential deductions for my NIL athletes. I cannot stress enough the importance of having a **solid** tax professional in your circle to help guide you through this. **Please note:** this list can change over time and is not a full comprehensive list.

- ➢ Promotional activities
- ➢ Physical conditioning
- ➢ Hairstyling and manicures (Let's face it . . . you're being paid for your image.)
- ➢ Legal fees
- ➢ Travel expenses, including flights, hotels, airfare, rental cars, etc.
- ➢ Branding
- ➢ Clothing (as it relates to maintaining your "professional image")
- ➢ Makeup
- ➢ Marketing
- ➢ Mileage
- ➢ Equipment & supplies, such as laptops, video & audio equipment, etc.
- ➢ Website hosting
- ➢ Dues & subscriptions
- ➢ Phone charges
- ➢ Internet

While many of these expenses are truly allowable, it is **critical** that you keep adequate records. The last thing you want to do is have a deduction disallowed because you failed to keep good records. There are several low-cost software programs, such as QuickBooks, that can assist here. Trust me when I say, it is worth it, and you cannot afford not to have a good tracking system in place. Other records you can keep include bank statements, receipts, invoices, and credit card statements.

It is recommended that you open a separate bank account to keep the business revenue and expenses separate from your personal.

PHYSICAL CONDITIONING

Physical conditioning can include anything that helps you maintain your body/image. This could include:

- Gym Memberships
- Massages
- Chiropractor visits
- Meal prep
- Fitness clothing & equipment
- Physical therapy
- Personal training

I know I threw a lot at you in a few short pages, but basically, NIL deals give you the opportunity to capitalize on your athletic fame. Just be aware of the rules the IRS has put in place. If you had to take anything from this section, know this: Some of you are gearing up to make a ton of money. As such, it is critical to do your homework upfront so you can enjoy the fruits of your hard work later. We want to make sure you understand how to **keep** a large chunk of that money that you have worked so hard for. Let's face it, that's what will help you and your family accumulate wealth. Wealth is not about how much money you make . . . It is about how much you **keep** and **grow**.

Consider speaking with a financial advisor to open a retirement account. Speak with the advisor and your tax professional to determine which type of account would be most beneficial to you. Some may help reduce your taxable income.

KEY TAKEAWAYS

1. When you are being paid for your image, conduct yourself accordingly, i.e., maintain a solid professional image.
2. Your name is your brand. Treat it as a business.
3. Structure your brand as a business that is your full-time job. Set up an LLC and find ways to pay yourself as an employee of your LLC.
4. Surround yourself with a solid team that you can trust. This should include and accountant, an attorney, and a financial advisor at a minimum.

QUESTIONS FOR REFLECTION

1. How has your life changed since NIL deals became popular?
2. Have you started building your business all-star team?

CHAPTER 6

BUDGETING 101

THE BLUEPRINT FOR KEEPING YOUR MONEY

> WHEN MONEY CONTROLS YOU, YOU ARE LIVING PAYCHECK TO PAYCHECK, YOU ARE STRESSED, AND YOU ARE ALWAYS WANTING MORE AND MORE MONEY.

We've spent a good amount of time focused on how to get money for school and how to make money while in school. Now that you have secured the bag, we will discuss how to **keep** that money and how to create a written plan for your money.

A budget is a written plan where you take control of your money by telling it where to go and not wondering where it went.
—John Maxwell

Creating a budget is a firm way to take control of your money. With a budget, you can tell your money exactly where to go, rather than looking back and wondering where it went. Budgeting does not have to be an intimidating task. Conversely, it is a necessary activity for individuals and families, regardless of age. I emphasize making this plan written because that will make it real to you. Writing your budget down helps you face reality and tackle it head-on. Budgeting is controlling your money and not letting it control you. There is a reason they call it *cash flow*: if you do not control it, then it will *flow* right on out of your home.

If you aim at nothing, you will hit it every time!
—Zig Ziglar

It is worth discussing the reasons that people choose not to budget. The fact that you are reading this chapter tells me you won't utilize any of these excuses along your journey:

X "It feels like being in a straitjacket."
X Their budget never worked.
X They are paralyzed by the fear of what they may find.

My absolute favorite budgeting story so far was when I sat down to help my friend (we'll call her Amber) "get her money together." Amber and I had spoken several times about her "money problems," and she watched all the videos I posted online. She constantly talked about how she was always living paycheck to paycheck and thought if she could just get a raise, her money problems would just magically be solved, like some genie in the bottle. I have seen Amber's approach hundreds of times. We think that more money will fix our financial issues. Let me be the first to tell you: More money will only magnify your financial troubles. What I mean is, if you have a trash relationship with money, then having more of it will simply compound those issues. But back to Miss Amber. She finally did get her raise, and she jumped for joy, bought a nice bottle of wine, and called me to share the good news. After getting a few of her new paychecks, we revisited our "paycheck-to-paycheck" conversation. She just could not figure out how on earth she was still struggling after a $20,000 raise. It made absolutely no sense to her, so we finally sat down to do her budget. As I pulled up to her house, I noticed a new car in the driveway. I asked, "Oh no, did your old car break down?" She answered, "No. I just wanted a new car. I got this raise, so I could afford it." Not wanting to kill her joy, I smiled and bit my tongue. As I turned to her living room, I noticed brand-new couches with the tags still on them! Again, I asked, "Did the kids finally jump through the couches?" She replied, "Nope. I could afford better ones now." By now, I was smiling because it was just as I had suspected. But I was there to help, so I just let her talk and walk me through her monthly spending. I told her, "Now's not the time to omit anything." It was time for us to have a very honest conversation. As we went through her zero-based budget (more on this later), there were several times she was completely shocked and almost fell out of her seat!

1. She had no idea she was spending over $200 per week at McDonald's. Yes, you read that correctly. And if that behavior goes unchecked for an entire year, she's spending $10,400 per year ($200 x 52 weeks) just at McDonald's!

   Imagine what $10,400 would look like sitting in an account earning 8% compound interest!

2. She did not realize that after all her expenses each week, she had an extra $150 she could invest or save. If you combine this with the "McDonald's fund" above, in a year's time, Amber could have saved or invested $14,300!

When my friend Amber realized these two facts, she could hardly believe what was staring back at her from that paper budget. She now understood just how important it is to address your financial shortcomings head-on and not be afraid of what you may be forced to address. Now, you may not end up with an extra $15K per year saved, but what you may realize is that you *can* take control of your money and turn your financial situation around . . . It just takes a little planning.

In this chapter, we will walk you through each step of the budgeting process so you can have a full budget plan ready to activate. And before you say that I'm telling you what to do with the money you have worked so hard for, let me stop you. I am merely providing you with a blueprint so you take charge of your hard-earned money. This plan will only work as well as the time and effort you are willing to put in. Creating the plan is only the first step. It is up to you to act.

> *A written plan removes the "management*
> *by crisis" from your finances.*
> *—Dave Ramsey*

I want to be very honest: budgeting will not start out as an easy process. But with repetition, it will become like second nature to you. I compare it to a baby learning how to walk. Imagine if that baby decided that walking wasn't for him/her after falling down a few times. We would be carrying that baby until they were full-grown adults. Learning to walk takes time and patience and a little perseverance.

> *If you can't fly then run, if you can't run then*
> *walk, if you can't walk then crawl, but whatever*
> *you do you have to keep moving forward.*
> *—Dr. Martin Luther King Jr.*

Now, I am quite positive that you do not want any more homework. However, this "homework" has the potential to change the entire trajectory of your financial life and the financial life of many generations after you. Budgeting is less about the actual numbers and more about the discipline of it. We like to use what is called *zero-based budgeting*. And before you freak out and say, "Dr. O is trying to make me spend all my money," just hear me out. The basis of zero-based budgeting is to allocate all your income down to zero (on paper) before you ever get paid. This is the written plan we discussed earlier. You write down the income you will receive and list every expense for that month. This should include your savings, giving, fun, shopping, etc. When you are done, that bottom line should be zero. It does not mean that you have no money left over. What a zero-based budget tells you is that you have accounted for every penny you have made. You have control of your money and have, with intention, told it exactly where it needs to go! What you may find is that you can afford to go to a nicer restaurant or buy those new shoes you have been wanting. You may have the exciting (and eye-opening) revelation that my friend Amber had.

It's *your* money. What you do with it is your business. Your decisions will not make or break me. (Trust me, I will be okay.) I just want you to be intentional about how you use it.

Next, we will get into the nitty-gritty of creating your own budget.

STEP 1: HOW DO YOU MAKE MONEY?

There are various ways to make money (legally, of course). This can be from a job (**E**mployment), self-employment (**S**), business ownership (**B**), and/or investments (**I**).

If you have not read *The Cashflow Quadrant* by Robert Kiyosaki, I highly recommend it. I won't go into great detail here, but I will show you what the Cashflow Quadrant looks like and how it can relate to your budget and financial health.

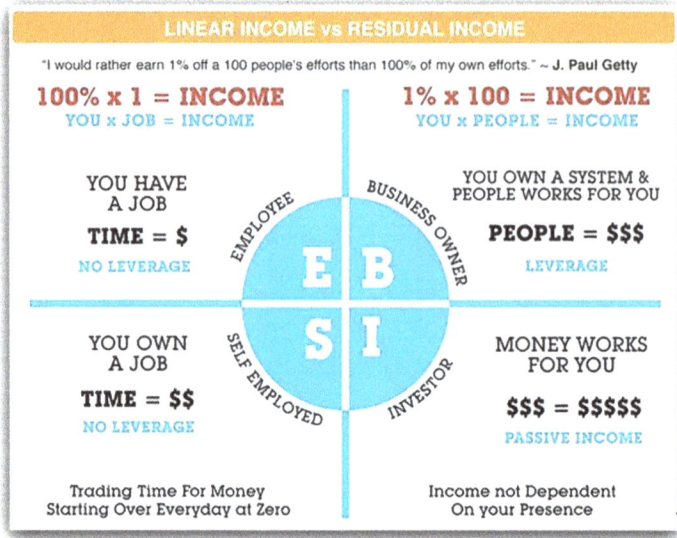

LINEAR INCOME vs RESIDUAL INCOME

"I would rather earn 1% off a 100 people's efforts than 100% of my own efforts." ~ J. Paul Getty

100% x 1 = INCOME
YOU x JOB = INCOME

1% x 100 = INCOME
YOU x PEOPLE = INCOME

YOU HAVE
A JOB

TIME = $

NO LEVERAGE

YOU OWN A SYSTEM &
PEOPLE WORKS FOR YOU

PEOPLE = $$$

LEVERAGE

EMPLOYEE   BUSINESS OWNER

E **B**

S **I**

SELF EMPLOYED   INVESTOR

YOU OWN
A JOB

TIME = $$

NO LEVERAGE

MONEY WORKS
FOR YOU

$$$ = $$$$$

PASSIVE INCOME

Trading Time For Money
Starting Over Everyday at Zero

Income not Dependent
On your Presence

In a nutshell, the Cashflow Quadrant demonstrates the different ways that we make money, the ways in which we can move from quadrant to quadrant, and how each quadrant makes money. No matter what your income "method" is, write it down. Be *intentional* (you will see me use this word quite often).

Income Source	Amount
Scholarship(s)	$
Work Study(ies)	$
Employment Income	$
Side Hustle 1	$
Side Hustle 2	$
Dividend (Investment) Income	$
Interest	$
Self-Employment Income	$
Total	$

STEP 2: WHERE IS YOUR MONEY GOING?

Beware of little expenses. A small
leak will sink a great ship.
—Benjamin Franklin

It is critical to understand exactly where you are prioritizing (spending) your money. This is a major step in taking full control of your hard-earned money. This is not the time to get cute and omit things. This is where you confront your spending habit head-on! This is personal, so don't be ashamed or afraid of what you may find. Know where that money is going, so you don't have to wonder where it went. Remember my friend Amber earlier? She could not figure out how she was burning through all her money, even after a raise. She had a small leak (McDonald's) that was literally sinking her because she had no idea where the leak was! If alcohol or weed are your vices, I am not here to condemn you morally. Put it in your budget. (It may be eye-opening enough to make you quit, LOL.)

Before spending money, ask yourself the following:
1. Can I afford it?
2. Do I really need it?
3. How will this purchase affect me?

Write down **every** expense you expect to have within your budget period (whether that's monthly, by semester, quarterly, or annually).

It's okay if you do not know how much you typically spend in certain areas. One way to check is to do a simple audit of your bank statements: open your banking app and see how much you spend on average in certain categories like Fast Food.

I like to separate my expenses into four major categories:

- **65% - Basic Necessities** (Food, Clothing, Shelter, Transportation)
- **10% - Giving**
- **15% - Saving & Investing**
- **10% - Fun/Personal**

Please note: These are just suggestions, and you are *allowed to have sub-categories, or play with the percentages.*

Investments

Credit Card Pmts

Leisure

Savings

Student Loan(s)

Tithes/Giving

Insurance

FUN

Groceries

Travel

Car Note

Dues/Subscriptions

Phone

Retirement

Shopping

Restaurants

Rent/Mortgage

Internet/Cable

Clothing

Utilities

STEP 3: YOUR BOTTOM LINE SHOULD BE ZERO.

And before you even think it, no, I am not telling you to spend all your money. That is not the goal. The goal is to have a plan for your money and know exactly where it is going to go before you spend it. Creating a zero-based budget allows you to assign a name and purpose to every dollar you make, whether that's investing, savings, necessities, fun, clothing, travel, etc. It does not matter where or how you spend it. What matters is proper planning and having that plan written.

Zero-Based Budget Example	
Scholarships (Refund)	$5,000.00
Work Study	$2,500.00
Other Jobs	$500.00
Total Income	**$8,000.00**
Basic Needs (65%)	
Rent	$2,500.00
Utilities	$ 750.00
Food	$ 600.00
Car Insurance & Gas	$1,100.00
Clothing	$ 250.00
Giving (10%)	**$ 800.00**
Saving & Investing (15%)	**$ 1,200.00**
FUN/Personal (10%)	
Going Out	$ 150.00
Hair & Nails	$ 500.00
Travel	$ 150.00
Total Expenses	**$8,000.00**
BOTTOM LINE (Income – Expenses)	**$ 0.00**

REASONS YOUR BUDGET WON'T WORK

1. You leave things out.
2. You make your plan 10x more complicated than it needs to be.
3. You don't take the time to actually do your budget.
4. You don't actually stick to your budget.

STEP 4: HOW CAN WE KEEP MORE OF OUR HARD-EARNED MONEY?

I'm not telling you to create a budget because I want you to cheat yourself, I'm telling you to create a budget because I want you to treat yourself.
—Dafina Sharpe

A. INCREASE YOUR INCOME

Now, of course we want to keep this increase as legal as humanly possible. I can tell you, from our conversation earlier in this text, that one way is to look for more scholarships. Although time may be a bit limited (since you are a student), look for ways you can monetize things you are already doing for free or things that bring you joy and a sense of satisfaction. Here are a few ways we teach people to find new ways to make money:

- **What are you passionate about?**
  Think through all the things you enjoy doing that could potentially turn into an added source of income. One thing I found myself doing for free was coaching local kids. I did it because I truly enjoyed it and the kids truly benefitted from my assistance. Over time, parents started asking to pay me for private lessons, which obviously added to my bottom line and put more cash into my pockets.

- **Listen to people whine about their problems.**
  There's a saying that goes, "Find a need and fill it!" How can you provide a solution to the problems people are complaining about? Most times you don't even need to speak—just listen. I assure you there are little nuggets out there, just waiting to be discovered. Don't record them (unless they agree to it), but write down the things you hear people complaining about. When you start to hear the same problems over and over, the likelihood of your sustained success with this business venture increases substantially.

- **Think about the things that are taking up your time for free.**
  I can give you a long list of things people are doing for free that they could potentially monetize. However, I won't bore you with that long list. Now, I am not saying that every little thing you do should make you money. Some things you should do for the pure joy and thrill of it. What I am telling you is to do a simple evaluation to determine if there is anything that could make you more money. If you are lifting weights or working out four hours a day,

six days a week, maybe consider modeling, bodybuilding, or being a fitness coach. If you are sitting around gossiping every chance you get, maybe consider starting a podcast, blog, or YouTube channel.

One last tidbit of advice on this: put your ego aside. When I was on a mission to make more money to achieve my dreams, there wasn't a lawn I wouldn't cut or a toilet I wasn't willing to clean to get to that goal. Yes, at times it did feel humiliating, but I had to remind myself that I was working for a *much* larger goal than my sometimes short-sighted mind would allow.

No one is above delivering pizza, cleaning toilets, and mopping floors. In your pursuit of financial freedom, you cannot have a big ego. Leave him at home. Do what you gotta do to get to that finish line! I never knock anyone's hustle: (1) it is none of my business, and (2) you are trying to be free. Who am I to knock your hustle or throw shade?

B. CUT EXPENSES

What can you afford to live without? This is an activity I love doing whenever I am speaking to groups about budgeting. I have everyone write down all of their expenses (what we did here in step 2). Don't leave anything out. Once you have everything written down, think about what expenses you can live without or reduce. With my friend Amber, this activity led her to eat way fewer McDoubles, which also led to a much healthier physical life for her. You may find that you have already done this activity, and that's okay! Do not feel obligated to find something. Just occasionally review your expenses to see if there are things you do not need or want. One of the most common culprits are subscriptions. There's a reason so many businesses are okay switching to a subscription model. What often happens is we sign up for a "too good to pass up" promotion, use the subscription for six months, and then forget about it. Meanwhile, we forget to turn off the auto-draft and keep paying for a subscription we aren't even using. So there's nothing wrong with taking a regular inventory of your monthly bills.

BUDGET

KEY TAKEAWAYS

1. A budget is a firm way to take control of your hard-earned money. Budgeting is telling your money where to go and not wondering where it went.
2. Your budget should be written and should be reviewed often.
3. Creating a zero-based budget allows you to assign a name and purpose to every dollar you make, whether that's investing, savings, necessities, fun, clothing, travel, etc.

QUESTIONS FOR REFLECTION

1. What are some LEGAL ways you can add some additional income?
   - ☐ What are you passionate about?
   - ☐ What things have you heard people complain about lately?
   - ☐ What activities are you currently engaged in that are taking up your time for FREE?
2. What expenses do you currently have that you can afford to cut out? The answer may be "none," but make sure you review this regularly.

CHAPTER 7

INVESTING

WHEN SHOULD I START?

Great question! Start as early as possible but only whenever you can understand the investments you are interested in. If you don't understand an investment well enough to teach it to someone else, then you probably should not do it. Let me repeat that . . . **If you do not understand an investment well enough to teach it to someone else, then you probably should not do it.** I know this sounds a bit extreme and like I am trying to steer you away from investing, but let me assure you that I am not. I want each and every person reading this book to find extreme wealth and have many investments. However, I want each of you to **do your homework**. There is nothing worse than jumping into an investment on a whim or because some Instagram or TikTok "guru" said it was a good investment, and losing every last penny. It is a sickening feeling to watch your hard-earned money evaporate right before your eyes all because you failed to do your homework and make sure you understand where you were parking your money.

So, before we get technical, let me tell you how I got started in the investing world. I want to show you that I truly do "practice what I preach." When I was in college, I purchased my first house *and* learned the stock market. I remember sitting in my Finance 101 class at Grambling State University. (I remember it like it was just yesterday.) I recall us discussing the stock market, investments, etc. at a very high level. As I sat there, I wondered to myself, "Where on earth has all this information been hiding, and how can I get started?" It is a frustrating feeling to sit and wonder just how "far behind" you are in your financial journey. (This is why I always caution students against comparing your situation to others'. You never know where people truly are in their journey.)

I recall turning to my classmate, who was a non-traditional student, and simply asking him if he invested and how he got started. Those two very simple and honest questions completely changed the trajectory of my financial future. He directed me to his financial adviser, who he spoke very highly of. I set up a meeting with her and told her I was a blank slate and ready to learn! She smiled and told me that was exactly what she wanted to hear and to feel free to reach out to her any time I needed guidance or some additional knowledge.

She had no idea what door she had opened, because I was constantly reading and constantly taking notes, so I could be prepared for every meeting she and I had in order to maximize our time together. She was extremely patient with me and guided me until I was ready to fly solo. She even called me the one time I made a very elementary investor mistake and calmly told me not to ever do that again (and explained to me why it was not a smart decision . . . oops). As I grew as an investor, we celebrated the small milestones, which kept me motivated and excited about learning. I continued investing in various companies, understanding how to properly invest and grow my portfolio. This goes back to what I said at the beginning of this section: only invest in things that you can understand well enough to teach to someone else—and I most certainly did that! I shared every bit of information I learned, every roadblock, and every milestone with anyone who would listen, and I later helped many of them begin their investment journey. Now, I don't proclaim to know every nuance about investing, nor do I understand every single investment. However, I must understand anything that I invest my hard-earned dollars in.

Anytime I send my dollars out, I want them to come back with many "friends."
—Kevin O'Leary, Mr. Wonderful

Once I was able to master my stock market investing (and, yes, I am still learning every single day), I decided I wanted to understand a different type of investing: real estate. I had heard so much about how most hyper-wealthy people have a pretty substantial real estate portfolio. According to a report from Knight Frank, high-net-worth investors have roughly 32% and 21% of their holdings in residential real estate and commercial properties, respectively. Naturally, I wanted to know what these individuals knew that so many of us hadn't quite grasped yet. So I buckled in and started asking questions and doing the research (much like my studying of the stock market). I literally went to Google and typed "steps to purchase my first house" and started making calls. I contacted a bank, who then recommended a realtor, and by my twenty-first birthday, I had purchased my first home. I will admit that I was initially *terrified*, but I am glad I went and took the plunge. I am glad I wasn't afraid to be vulnerable and ask questions. I have shared my early investment stories with you to instill hope. I grew up in small-town

Grambling, Louisiana, and just dared to dream big and step outside of my comfort zone to get the things I wanted. And guess what? You can (and will) too!

INVESTING

Before you ever start investing in anything, it is important to understand the difference between assets and liabilities and how each affects your bottom line. Simply put, an *asset* is something that puts money into your pocket, while a *liability* takes money out of your pocket. It is imperative to understand the difference between an asset and a liability so you can determine if you are entering into a solid investment. You would be surprised how many people purchase a liability thinking that it will somehow magically be a good investment and make them some money. I cannot stress enough how important it is to know the difference.

> *Rich people acquire assets. The poor and middle class acquire liabilities, but they think they are assets.*
> *—Robert Kiyosaki, Rich Dad Poor Dad*

So what exactly *is* investing? Simply put, investing is when you use your money to buy something you anticipate will grow in value over time. According to Robert Kiyosaki in *The Cashflow Quadrant*, "Investors make money with money. They do not have to work because their money is working for them." Investing doesn't have to be an intimidating or boring topic at all. In fact, it should be fun. Think about how much fun the age-old game of Monopoly is. A simple childhood game has the potential to teach us so much about investing, if we pay close enough attention.

If people hope someday to be rich, they ultimately must come to the Investor Quadrant. It is in the "I" quadrant that money becomes converted to wealth.
—Robert Kiyosaki in The CASHFLOW Quadrant

At the end of the day, don't just hand your money over to a savvy advisor and walk away. Check in with them, schedule regular meetings with them, ask questions, actually look at your statements. Every successful person understands this small principle: surround yourself with people smarter than you, but you make the decisions. A good financial advisor will advise you but not force you into a decision. Remember that. It's your money; make sure you are the shot caller.

STOCKS

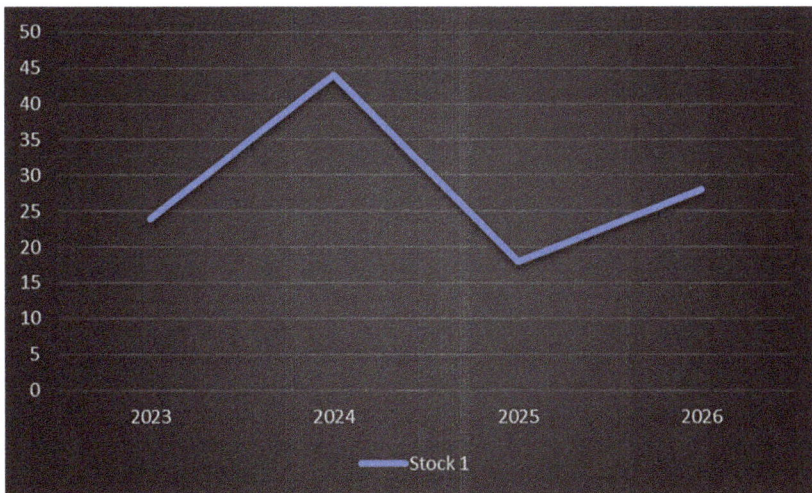

Stocks are one of the most common and well-known investments. I am more than positive that everyone reading this book has at least heard the term. So why the fascination with stocks and the stock market? A stock in a company represents a share of ownership in a company. A company (let's say Walmart) sells shares of their company to raise money. As a shareholder (the person who owns the stock), you want the stock to go up in price (or *appreciate*) over time. If, and when, a stock appreciates, you can sell the stock on the secondary market. For the sake of this book, we will not go into too much detail about the secondary market, options, etc. We just want to provide you with a basic understanding with which you can begin your investing journey. Another key benefit of stock ownership is the potential income from dividends that the company may pay (more on this later). Stocks can be purchased through a broker at a bank or other financial institution or through various online platforms like E-Trade (one I have used since college). One thing to note about stocks is this: They *will* fluctuate over time. That is the dynamic of the market. It is constantly moving, up, down, and sideways. You have buyers, and you have sellers . . . supply and demand. That's what makes stocks so fun!

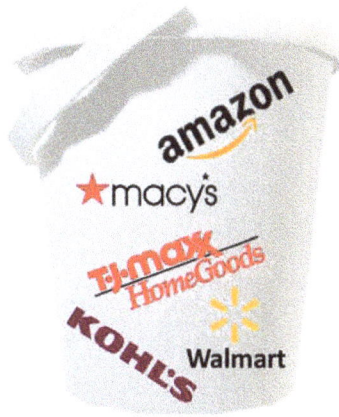

MUTUAL FUNDS

Stocks are not the only form of investing. In fact, some may literally get nauseous even thinking about the rollercoaster ride that is the stock market. Many beginning investors may go with a much safer investment, such as mutual funds. I, too, started out with a portfolio of mutual funds before I dove into individual stock investing. Mutual fund investing is a much safer way to "get your feet wet" while learning more about the markets. So how and why are mutual funds so safe? To answer this question, it is important to understand what exactly mutual funds are.

A mutual fund is a pool of several assets that allows investors to invest in several different assets, such as stocks and bonds. You may have a mutual fund of grocery stocks holding companies like Walmart. These mutual funds are safe because they allow you to take ownership in several different companies for a fraction of the cost. The performance of a mutual fund is based on the assets (typically stocks and bonds) within that fund. Mutual funds have managers who are responsible for keeping an eye on the performance of each fund in the mutual fund. When an asset is underperforming, the manager replaces it with a better asset. Mutual funds take advantage of a term called *diversification* and are an excellent investment option when you don't have access to as much money. Here's an example: As of the date of this book, one share of Walmart will cost you roughly $78. Conversely, investing that same $78 in a mutual fund will buy you fractional shares of Walmart and several other companies within that particular fund.

TRADING & INVESTING ARE NOT THE SAME

I am pretty sure many of you have seen all the TikTok "experts" giving advice about joining their networks of traders so you can become a millionaire in the next five years. I am not saying this is not possible. Believe me, there are some that do win big when they are trading in the market. However, they take extremely high risks in order to achieve high rewards. So, again, I am not one to knock anyone's hustle, nor will I tell you that it does not work. What I am here to tell you is that there is a huge difference between trading and investing and the two should *not* be used interchangeably. The main difference is **timelines** and **objectives**. Both traders and investors, obviously, intend to make money. Traders buy and sell assets **frequently (many times daily or weekly)**, with their main focus being on **short-term gains**. Conversely, investing involves buying and holding assets for **longer periods of time**. Investors focus on long-term gains to help pay for things like retirement and college. While trading can be fun and even addicting, never use trading as a long-term retirement strategy. You want retirement investments to pay over time and be a little safer than the constant, quick asset movement associated with trading.

COMPOUND INTEREST: TIME IS ON YOUR SIDE

Albert Einstein referred to compound interest as the Eighth Wonder of the World. To understand compound interest, it is best to understand the difference between simple and compound interest.

Simple Interest	Compound Interest
Interest is paid on the principal only.	Interest is paid on the principal *and* on interest previously earned.
Example:	**Example:**
$200 invested at a rate of 10% for 3 years.	$200 invested at a rate of 10% for 3 years.
Year 1: Interest = $20 Year 2: Interest = $20 Year 3: Interest = $20	Year 1: Interest = $20 Year 2: Interest = $220 x 10% = $22 Year 3: Interest = $242 x 10% = $24.20
Total Interest Paid = **$60.00**	Total Interest Paid = **$66.20**

Let's see how this can impact your real money over your working lifetime.

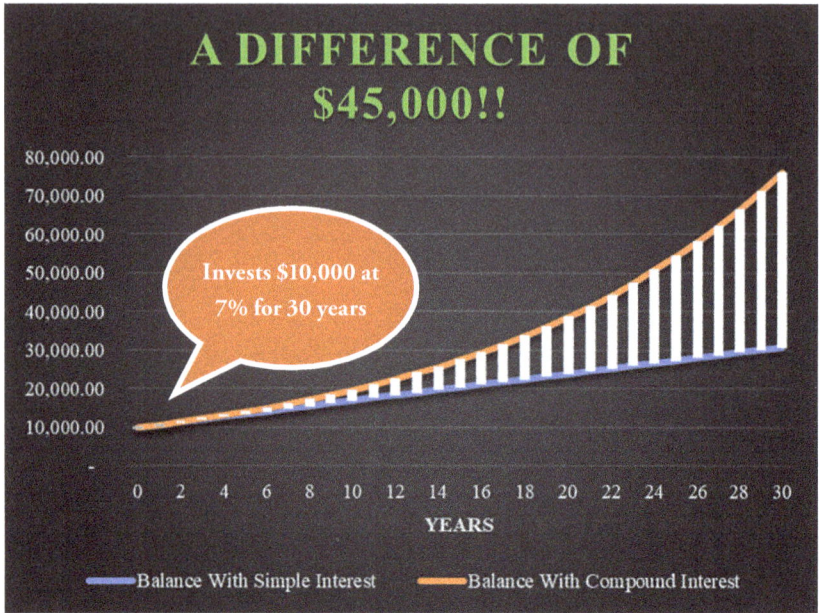

Interest	7%	per year
	Simple interest earned	Compound interest earned
Initial Deposit	10,000.00	10,000.00
Year 1	700.00	700.00
Year 2	700.00	749.00
Year 3	700.00	801.43
Year 4	700.00	857.53
Year 5	700.00	917.56
Year 6	700.00	981.79
Year 7	700.00	1,050.51
Year 8	700.00	1,124.05
Year 9	700.00	1,202.73
Year 10	700.00	1,286.92
Year 11	700.00	1,377.01
Year 12	700.00	1,473.40
Year 13	700.00	1,576.53
Year 14	700.00	1,686.89
Year 15	700.00	1,804.97
Year 16	700.00	1,931.32
Year 17	700.00	2,066.51
Year 18	700.00	2,211.17
Year 19	700.00	2,365.95
Year 20	700.00	2,531.57
Year 21	700.00	2,708.78
Year 22	700.00	2,898.39
Year 23	700.00	3,101.28
Year 24	700.00	3,318.37
Year 25	700.00	3,550.66
Year 26	700.00	3,799.20
Year 27	700.00	4,065.15
Year 28	700.00	4,349.71
Year 29	700.00	4,654.19
Year 30	700.00	4,979.98
Total Interest Earned	21,000.00	66,122.55

A Difference of $45,122.55

DIVIDENDS

Dividends are a percentage of a company's earnings paid to its shareholders. Simply put, it is your reward for holding a company's stock. Dividends can be paid in cash or additional shares in the company. Not all companies pay dividends, but it is relatively simple to identify which companies pay regular dividends and which don't. Now that we understand what dividends are, let's discuss how dividends relate to compound interest and a long-term investment strategy.

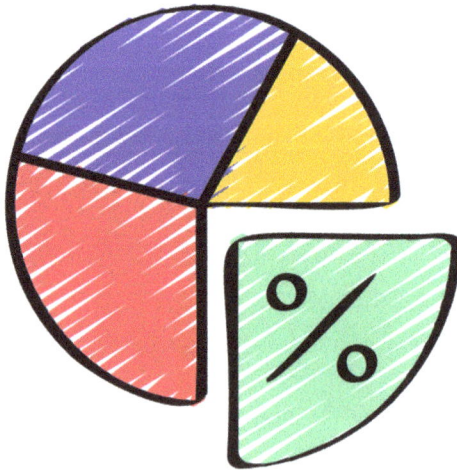

DRIP (DIVIDEND REINVESTMENT PLAN)

DRIPs are a different type of compound interest (and my absolute favorite). With DRIPs, instead of shareholders receiving their cash dividends, the investor's dividends are reinvested to purchase more stocks in the company. Over time, you can snowball the dividend reinvestments. The more shares you own, the more dividends you will receive.

LET'S LOOK AT AN EXAMPLE

You own 500 shares of Company A. The company's board of directors agrees to pay $2 per share. If you hold these 500 shares until a specified date, then you will receive $1,000. Prior to receiving this dividend, you can choose to receive a cash dividend deposited into your account or enroll in a DRIP. If you enroll in a DRIP, then you will receive let's say 10 more shares. You now have 510 shares of Company A. If the Board continues to pay the $2 dividend the following year, you will receive $1,020 (510 shares x $2 dividend) or if you enrolled in a DRIP (my recommendation), you will receive 10.2 shares. You now own 520.2 shares of Company A. If this continues, you can see the real-time effects of compound interest, in the form of dividend reinvestments.

KEY TAKEAWAYS

1. Start investing as early as possible.
2. The "right time" to start investing isn't associated with an age or number.
3. Only invest in things that you understand well enough to teach to someone else.
4. A mutual fund is a pool of several assets that allows investors to invest in several different assets, such as stocks and bonds, at the same time. Mutual funds are considered "safe" because they are diversified across several assets. When an asset is underperforming, the mutual fund manager replaces it with a better asset.
5. Compound interest is interest-on-interest, meaning interest is paid on the principal investment *and* the interest previously earned.

QUESTIONS FOR REFLECTION

1. What investments have you researched lately?
2. Is there any particular investment that you feel you understand enough to teach someone else?
3. What investment experience do you currently have?
4. Would you prefer a cash dividend or a DRIP? Why?

CHAPTER 8

MAKING THE MOST OF THE COLLEGE EXPERIENCE

"We party hard…
We stay up late…
But most of all, we graduate!"

We've spent a great deal of time discussing the following:

1. How to get into college.
2. How to pay for college.
3. How to keep your money while in college.
4. How and when to start investing, while in college.

But what about the things you need to do while *in* college that will help you *stay* in college and graduate with a plan in place? I am sure many of you, like me, were ready to go to college to leave the care and strict rules of your parents' home and party, party, party. Am I right, or am I right? Now, while I agree that you should 100% enjoy yourself while in college and make some really good memories and funny stories (I certainly have plenty of those), let's remember the main reason that you are there: to get an education (hopefully for free) and to graduate! My fraternity has a saying, "We party hard . . . we stay up late . . . but most of all we graduate!" In this chapter, we will discuss some steps you can and should take to set yourself up for ultimate success during and, most importantly, after college.

ENJOY THE COLLEGE EXPERIENCE (WITHIN REASON)

I will be the first to tell you: college *should* be an experience. You should meet new people, try new things, travel to the big rivalry games (the Bayou Classic for us), and make a million memories that you can one day tell your grandkids over and over. No one will ever fault you for enjoying your time in school. Honestly, I wish someone had told me to have fun and not worry so much about "adulting." My mother used to always tell me that I had the rest of my life to work and make money, but as most kids do, I thought I knew better than my parents. (Ha-ha, joke's on me.) I worked, made a bunch of money, and bought a bunch of stuff, but it wasn't until my senior year that I realized I was missing out on the whole college experience. Thankfully, it wasn't too late, and I had that last year to enjoy—and I did just that. However, I always remembered that I was ultimately there to graduate and I could not allow anything to jeopardize that.

I tell you that story so you can understand that college is the time to make memories and be a college student. Will you make mistakes? Of course! Is it the end of the world? No, it is not! Enjoy the ride, but remember to surround yourself with people who will make you better in some aspect of your life, i.e., physical, emotional, educational, spiritual, etc.

MAINTAIN YOUR GRADES

At the end of the day, the only way to graduate is by maintaining a certain GPA. Every school has a requirement, and I suggest you know your school's. You would be surprised how many young people go to college with a super-high GPA, decide to pledge a fraternity or sorority or party hard and simply live it up, only to find they're literally flunking right out of school. By then, they have already lost their scholarship(s) and will have to take out loans or drop out of school. Please do not put yourself or your parents through that level of stress. You have worked extremely hard to get into college and, in many cases (hopefully after reading this book), obtained scholarships to help pay for it. Don't lose it all because you lost focus. Have fun, but remember *why* you are there.

DEVELOP RELATIONSHIPS (APPROPRIATELY, OF COURSE) WITH YOUR PROFESSORS

One thing every one of my professors will tell you is that I definitely utilized their office hours. If I had a question about the one question I missed on a test, they would get a knock on their doors during their designated office hours. I can recall very vividly one of my professors chuckling one day when he saw me coming and saying, "You are the *last* one who needs to be in here worried about a grade, but I admire your drive." He was referring to me asking about having a 98% instead of 100. It seems ridiculous, but have you met my parents? (LOL)

What this created was a very trusting relationship where my professors *always* had my back and were running over each other to write recommendation letters for jobs and graduate school. I wasn't a computer information systems major, but everyone in the Grambling College of Business knew Dr. Poe. He developed solid relationships with his students and ensured they were in a position to win. Many of my friends have him to thank for landing them several internship and job opportunities throughout school and after.

CHOOSE A MAJOR THAT WILL LAND YOU A SOLID JOB

We all know that the career you chose back in fifth grade is probably not what you will be doing ten years later. We get it. Life is a constant journey, and college is no different. While you are trying to figure out this "adulting" thing, you still have to start thinking about life after college. It may be easy to pick the "easy" majors or general studies. However, what jobs do you think you will land with a general studies degree? College majors aren't the be-all-end-all, but it most certainly helps when your major aligns with your career choice. I am not saying that you have to choose a major or career *today*, but what I am saying is to choose *wisely*. Start researching careers that not only bring you fulfillment but also can make you some money over your lifetime.

APPLY FOR INTERNSHIPS REGULARLY

We spoke about this earlier in this book, but it was so important that it is definitely worth repeating. Internships can open up a whole new world for you during and after college. Many internships will bring you on full-time during the summer (and pay you) and then maintain a relationship with you throughout the school year (externships). The cool thing about internships is that once a company has started investing in you, they typically will want a return on that investment. If you do a good job, then that "return" is the company converting you to a full-time employee after graduation. So make sure you intern often and maintain those relationships with the employers. Stay in communication with the recruiter(s) and apply for their internships each year and jobs once graduation is approaching.

BUILD YOUR RESUME

Your resume is your professional snapshot. It tells prospective employers who you are educationally and professionally. Every student should have one. Consider building your resume as soon as possible.

Note: Be careful not to go overboard. The last thing an employer wants is to have to spend days reading through your resume. Make your resume clear, concise, and easy to read. Many schools have free resources in your career development area. They will not only help you craft a good resume, but also help you apply for internships and jobs. Make sure you tap in often. I cannot stress enough to use this resource.

BE CAREFUL WHAT YOU ARE POSTING

Your social media and internet presence are your unofficial resume. I get that you want to take pictures and videos to remember all the fond memories you are making. However, everything is not worth posting. While your drunk friend in the dorm bathroom may make some funny memories, posting a drunken photo to social media may hurt them later when they are trying to get a job. Your social media presence can be viewed as your personal brand, and you must protect your brand at all costs. Many HR professionals do check your online presence. Don't let one fun night ruin your professional future.

COLLEGE SHOULD PREPARE YOU FOR THE REAL WORLD – GOVERN YOURSELF ACCORDINGLY

Those who knew me during my days at Grambling State University and the University of Arkansas can tell you that I showed up to class every day like it was my full-time job (because, technically, it was). I showed up in a suit or at least a shirt and tie. Imagine a nineteen-year-old kid showing up in a suit and tie *daily*. Why did I do this when everyone else was in sweats and/or pajamas? Well, my mother always taught me that you never know who you may encounter while you are outside of your home. The first time people see you is often how you will be remembered. They will remember how you looked, how you talked, how you smelled, and how you made them feel. Oftentimes, when you are on a college campus, you will cross paths with a recruiter. Sometimes, they may be sitting in your classroom when you walk in, and trust me, they notice who is there on time and who shows up late. I'm not telling you to go out and buy a new wardrobe, but I am telling you to make a good impression on everyone you encounter on that campus.

CHAPTER 9

WHY COLLEGE IS NOT FOR EVERYONE

know, I know, I know. This seems completely contradictory to everything we have discussed throughout this book, right? Just hear me out for a sec. Earlier in this book, I mentioned how I began my college career as a forensic chemistry major before later switching my major to business and finance. Why am I telling you this? Well, here's the thing. Part of why I switched majors is because I could not imagine going to school for four years (or more) just to get into a career that I hated. Your happiness is more important than any level of education you may attain. Think about it. Think about how many unhappy people you have encountered, who appear to hate everything about the job they're doing. When you enjoy the work you do and going to work every day, then your product/service will reflect that. You will put your best foot forward. And let's face it: Times have most certainly changed from when I was growing up. We were always taught to go be doctors, lawyers, judges, and any other glamorous title you could imagine. It all sounded like excellent planning and a surefire road to success. However, as we got older and knew people in these career fields, we started to realize how stressful their paths were and the glaring mound of debt that would haunt them for a large part of their careers. At the time of this publication, medical school debt is greater than $200,000, while law school debt tops $130,000! And let's face it, most don't graduate and immediately step into a career paying enough to eliminate their loan debt payments. After interest on those loans, students are looking at almost double those amounts! So why go into a career you aren't 100% happy in while accumulating so much debt all because "someone told you it was the smart way"?

Conversely, there are several other options available. If finding a trade is what brings you the most joy, then (like Nike says) just do it! Don't believe me? Allow me to provide an example or two. During my adult life, I have had the "privilege" of having some plumbing done. Has anyone reading this book ever looked at a plumbing bill? Most plumbers charge between $45 and $200 per hour! Imagine that! Our generation was always steered far away from trades like plumbing, when, let's face it, everyone needs a plumber! Another example: welders. I challenge you to go research welding jobs to see how much it costs to get certifications and subsequently how much welding jobs are paying. Currently, welders can expect to be paid anywhere from $29,000 to $54,000 per year. These may not be the super-glamorous titles you have been taught to go after. But, when you think about it (a) you get to be happy, and (b) you don't have to worry about repaying a mountain of student-loan debt and can start your life with no strings attached and on a leveled playing field.

Go chase your dreams and happiness, and the money will most certainly follow. I am glad that I switched career paths. Every day, I get to wake up and do exactly what I enjoy and help people. Because my clients can see how much I enjoy helping them and how much time I invest in perfecting my craft, they are more willing to pay my price and are more inclined to refer me to their colleagues.

KEY TAKEAWAYS

1. There are alternate paths to financial freedom. College is not the only way.
2. Consider learning a trade. It is a much cheaper alternative, and if it is what will bring you true happiness (and freedom), then go for it!

QUESTIONS FOR REFLECTION

1. What is your dream job?
2. If money was not an issue, would you pursue your dream job?
3. Do you feel obligated to attend college?

WE COVERED A LOT TODAY. SO WHERE DO I START?

Allow me to leave you with this story about my very first client. I had known this gentleman his entire life. It wasn't until 2007 that I started working with him to fix his financial woes. At the time, this gentleman was a college student. He came from a two-parent household with both parents completing advanced degrees. He has five siblings and grew up in a very small town. His lightbulb moments came twice before we began our journey:

1. Prior to attending college, he asked his parents to utilize his college fund since he was receiving full-ride scholarships. Their response to him was eye-opening: "Son, what college fund?"
2. As he sat in his college finance class one day (in a classroom like many of you), he turned to his classmate, who was a non-traditional student, and asked, "How in the world do people invest and make money? What is it that I am missing that has some of my peers inheriting land, assets, etc?"

These two questions led him into deep thought, which led to our collaborative relationship. Over the next fifteen years, I worked with this young man, teaching him literally everything I learned along my journey: How to budget, how to save for retirement, how to pay off bad debt, how to leverage banks to acquire assets, how to purchase businesses, the difference between an asset and a liability, and the list goes on. As I learned, he learned. He learned to budget, invest, save for his and his family's futures, and more! I think I may have enjoyed the journey and his growth just as much as he did!

That person is Clement Ogunyemi. Yes, you guessed it . . . that's *me*. I say this to say that everyone starts somewhere. Sometimes we have to be okay looking in the mirror and coming to grips with the fact that it's your finances, and the only person who can fix your money is you! Sometimes the only person holding you back is you. So look in the mirror and tell yourself, "I am in control! I can do this! I *will* fix my finances!"

Here is a poem that has reminded me to just . . . keep . . . going!

DON'T QUIT

When things go wrong, as they sometimes will,
when the road you're trudging seems all uphill,
when the funds are low and the debts are high,
and you want to smile but you have to sigh,
when care is pressing you down a bit –
rest if you must, but don't you quit.

Life is queer with its twists and turns.
As everyone of us sometimes learns.
And many a fellow turns about
when he might have won had he stuck it out.
Don't give up though the pace seems slow –
you may succeed with another blow.

Often the goal is nearer than
it seems to a faint and faltering man;
Often the struggler has given up
when he might have captured the victor's cup;
and he learned too late when the night came down,
how close he was to the golden crown.

Success is failure turned inside out –
the silver tint of the clouds of doubt,
and when you never can tell how close you are,
it may be near when it seems afar;
so stick to the fight when you're hardest hit –
it's when things seem worst, you must not quit.

—*Edgar Albert Guest*

If you can't fly then run,
if you can't run then walk,
if you can't walk then crawl,
but whatever you do you have
to keep moving forward.
—Dr. Martin Luther King Jr.

THE FINANCIAL LITERACY PLEDGE

I, _____, hereby pledge my entire being to developing a better financial future for myself, my family, and future generations to come.

Beginning today, I will make informed financial decisions, understanding the difference between wants and needs. I will consciously be aware of the effects of advertisements on my decision-making process and resolve not to be influenced by them. I will focus on my financial health by tracking my expenses and creating a budget that is realistic.

I will continue my education about personal debt, saving, investing, budgeting, and credit. I will be proactive in my planning for periodic expenses, including holidays. I will lead by example, teaching my children the importance of expense management, saving, budgeting, and the wise use of credit. I will no longer let fear and shame prevent me from talking about my financial well-being and seeking the necessary help to fix it.

From this day forth, I will not make excuses for my behavior and will no longer make poor financial decisions.

Signed: _____

Date: _____

*Today's the day I start my
journey to financial freedom!
No more excuses . . .
No more procrastination . . .
I want wealth!
I want prosperity!
I want comfort!
I want freedom!*

COLLEGE SELECTION WORKSHEET

What school(s) do I want to attend?	
How much does it cost to attend this/these school(s)?	
How will I pay for my education?	
Have I applied to these schools?	
If so, have I received a response?	

COLLEGE PREPAREDNESS CHECKLIST

High School Freshman

- ☐ Get involved! Start doing your community service and extra-curricular activities. Make sure you document what you do for these organizations.
- ☐ Take practice ACT/SAT exams.
- ☐ Identify schools you are interested in (list does not have to be final). Make sure you write down their entrance criteria and the financial aid they offer.
- ☐ Parents: If you haven't already, start your child's college fund.

High School Sophomore

- ☐ Take your first swing at the ACT/SAT. (Don't worry, you have two more years to increase your score).
- ☐ Start researching scholarships. There are no limits to your search. Look for any and all scholarships that you may qualify for (economic, academic, sports, military, etc.). Keep good records of every scholarship you apply for.
- ☐ Continue building your list of schools you are interested in.

High School Junior

- ☐ Consider taking another stab at the ACT/SAT test.
- ☐ Start applying for entry into your ideal colleges.
- ☐ Research the costs of your ideal school(s).

- ☐ What type of financial aid do your ideal schools provide?
- ☐ Continue scholarship research and begin applying for scholarships.
- ☐ Be on the lookout for college acceptance and recruiting letters.

High School Senior

- ☐ If you did not achieve your target test scores, retake your ACT/SAT.
- ☐ Fill out FAFSA.
- ☐ Apply for colleges and universities.
- ☐ Apply for financial aid.
- ☐ If tuition plus financial aid is less than ideal, look into junior college/community college to knock out your core classes for a much lower price. Note: Before you begin, make sure the credits will transfer to the college you want to attend.
- ☐ Make sure your mailing address is up-to-date with the schools and scholarships you have applied for.
- ☐ Be on the lookout for college acceptance letters and scholarship letters.

College Freshman

- ☐ Knockout core classes.
- ☐ Keep your grades up!
- ☐ Look into freshmen scholarships available at your school.
- ☐ Apply for external freshmen scholarships.

College Sophomore

- ☐ Maintain a solid GPA.
- ☐ Update your resume.
- ☐ Attend career fairs.

- ☐ Apply for internships.
- ☐ Apply for work-study programs within your field.

College Junior

- ☐ If you haven't already, declare a major.
- ☐ Attend career fairs and job fairs.
- ☐ Apply for internships.
- ☐ Apply for externships.
- ☐ Update your resume.
- ☐ Join a professional organization that will help you build your resume, apply for jobs, prepare for the workforce, etc.
- ☐ Apply for work-study programs within your field.
- ☐ Apply for scholarships for college juniors at your school.
- ☐ Apply for external scholarships.
- ☐ If you attended junior college/community college, look into transfer student scholarships.

College Senior

- ☐ Maintain a solid GPA.
- ☐ Apply for externships.
- ☐ Update your resume.
- ☐ Start applying for jobs (for after graduation).
- ☐ Apply for work-study programs within your field.
- ☐ Last chance to apply for more scholarships.

SAVING FOR COLLEGE

It is true that **p**roper **p**reparation **p**romotes **p**rosperity! It is critical to put together a written plan to prepare yourself for college, so let's start our journey with the end in mind. What I mean by this is that we must determine how much it will cost us to go to college (in the future) so that we can start saving today.

Now, let's assume that you are putting your money into a solid mutual fund (hint, hint) so it can grow over time. As of the date of this publication, Morningstar shows the average mutual fund returns over the last fifteen years (across all fund classes) is roughly **7.94%**. **Please note:** Some fund classes have much higher returns. Always consult a financial advisor.

A study by CollegeBoard data showed that in 2022, the average annual tuition for public, four-year colleges was $10,740 for in-state students and $27,560 for out-of-state students. Add to that the average cost of room and board of roughly $11,950, and the total average annual cost for an out-of-state student is **$39,510**. We used the out-of-state tuition costs since we wanted to plan conservatively.

HOW MUCH YOU NEED TO SAVE

Now that we know how much college can cost per year on average, let's calculate how much you need to save per month.

The annual cost of college (average) =   *$39,510*

× 4 years =   *$158,040*

Now, let's do the math here:

Amount needed to save for college =   *$158,040*

X factor below (Let's assume you're 8 years old.) =   **X 0.005466**

Monthly Savings Needed =   **$ 863.85**

8% FACTORS (SELECT THE 1 THAT MATCHES YOUR AGE)		
AGE	*YEARS TO SAVE*	*8% FACTOR*
0	18	0.002083
2	16	0.002583
4	14	0.003247
6	12	0.004158
8	10	0.005466
10	8	0.007470
12	6	0.010867
14	4	0.017746

SCHOLARSHIP SEARCH TRACKER

Scholarship Name	Scholarship Amount	Criteria (GPA, extracurricular, etc.)	1-Time or recurring?	If recurring, how many years?

RICH VS. WEALTHY – WHICH DO YOU PREFER?

Rich	Wealthy
Million-dollar main home	Million-dollar income-producing property
Leased Lamborghini	Owned Toyota Camry
6-figure checking account	7-figure brokerage & retirement accounts
Planning vacations	Living on vacation
Working for money	Money does all the work
Employer income	Passive income
Money is everything	Money is objective
Worried about how much money is **made**	Concerned with how much money is **kept**

GLOSSARY OF FINANCIAL TERMS

529 plan (also known as a qualified tuition program) – state-sponsored investment account that allows you to save money for education expenses.

asset – something that you own (puts money into your pockets).

bear market – stock market prices are falling, encouraging selling; opposite: bull market.

borrower – person who takes out debt; must repay the debt with interest.

bull market – stock market prices are rising, encouraging buying; opposite: bear market.

capital – money needed to produce goods and services.

capital gain – the profit from the sale of an asset (purchase price minus selling price); higher selling price, lower purchase price.

compound interest – interest paid on the original cash amount plus interest earned from previous periods (accumulated interest); interest on interest.

consumer – someone who buys goods and services for consumption from a producer.

debt – money borrowed by one person (borrower) to another (lender).

diversification – a mix (variety) of investments used to lower (mitigate) an investor's risk.

dividend – cash or stock rewards paid from a company's profits to its shareholders.

earned income – money made from working a job.

equity – percentage ownership of an asset or business. Note: when you have equity in a company, you own a piece of that company.

FAFSA (Free Application for Federal Student Aid) – form completed by students each year to determine their eligibility for financial assistance/aid.

future value – how much your money will be worth in the future. Note: this is where compound interest is important. $100 today will not be worth $100 in ten years.

gross pay – amount you are paid for the goods and services you provide. Note: this is the amount the company pays you before taxes are paid.

income – money coming into your home; examples: earned income, investment income, rental income.

inflation – prices of goods and services increase or the value of money decreases.

interest – the **penalty** for borrowing money; must be paid in addition to original loan amount, e.g., 7% interest. Note: you can charge interest on money that you "loan" to a bank (savings account) or to an individual.

internship – professional learning experience that integrates knowledge and theory learned in the classroom with practical applications and skills development in a professional environment.

investment – money used to buy assets that will be worth more in the future (appreciate).

investment income – money received from assets you have purchased; e.g., stocks

lender – person who loans money to another person, who then pays the money back plus interest.

leverage – using debt (borrowed money) to complete a project or pay for an investment.

liability – something that you owe (takes money out of your pockets).

liquidity – how easily your assets (things you own) can be sold for cash.

loan – something borrowed; must be repaid with interest. Principle plus interest = loan total.

money – used to trade for goods or services.

mortgage – money borrowed from the bank (loan) to purchase a home.

mutual fund – a diversified investment that pools together stocks, bonds, and other securities. Note: it allows investors that may not have a lot of money to invest in several different companies.

net pay – the money that you take home after paying taxes, also called "take-home pay."

net worth – assets (what you own) minus liabilities (what you owe). Note: we all want a positive net worth.

Pell Grant – a form of need-based financial aid awarded by the US Department of Education. These grants are awarded to low-income students to help supplement the costs of going to college (such as books, housing, tuition and fees, etc.).

producer – someone who grows or supplies goods for sale to a consumer.

rental income – money made from a piece of property that you own and rent to someone else (a tenant).

return on investment (ROI) – gain or loss on money that you invested.

risk – the chance of losing your money.

save – money you earn but do not spend. Note: make sure your savings account is an account that accumulates interest.

scholarship – a form of financial assistance/aid awarded to a student to pursue higher education. Scholarships are typically based on either academic achievement or other preset criteria such as community service or merit. Criteria is usually set by the person or entity giving that scholarship. Note: you do not have to repay scholarships (unless, in rare cases, you fail to meet specific criteria).

Securities and Exchange Commission (SEC) – the "stock police" – created to regulate the stock market and protect investors.

shareholder – person or company that owns stock (or shares) in a company.

simple interest – interest paid on the original cash amount only. Note: see *compound interest*.

stock – a company provides people with the opportunity to buy ownership in the company (called *shares*). Note: when you own stock in a company, you can vote on important issues of that company like their board of directors.

stockbroker – person who buys stocks from one person and sells to another – "the middle man."

stock market – the virtual store where people buy and sell stock ownership shares.

taxes – money paid to the government when you make money (income). Note: taxes are a percentage of the income you make.

volatility – how much and how quickly an investment's price changes.

work-study program – part-time jobs for undergraduate and graduate students who have demonstrated a financial need. The work-study program allows you to earn money that can be used to help pay for your educational expenses.

Dr. Clement Ogunyemi, The Finance Doctor, earned his Bachelor of Science degree in Business Management & Economics from Grambling State University. He then completed his MBA in Finance and Doctor of Business Administration, with a concentration in Finance, both from Walden University. His doctoral study focused on the strategies mortgage loan executives need to better prequalify mortgage loan applicants. Dr. O founded 4Q Pro Financial Management & Consulting to assist individuals and organizations to achieve their financial goals and ultimately achieve financial freedom and independence. He has grown 4Q Pro Financial to a multi-state operation, now operating in 4 states since its inception. Additionally, he has mentored NIL athletes on maximizing their NIL earnings, while saving on taxes. Dr. O has realized success as an outstanding CFO to nonprofit organizations in more than 10 states. Dr. O is also an avid real estate investor and has grown his portfolio over 7 figures. Dr. O is a philanthropist, who founded and serves as the President of the Ogunyemi Family Foundation, where he has increased scholarship giving by 33% annually. He also serves on several Non-Profit Boards, including the Narrows Institute of Biomedical Research & Education, the Voices of Diversity, the March of Dimes and NextGen Guidance.

www.ingramcontent.com/pod-product-compliance
Lightning Source LLC
Chambersburg PA
CBHW040902210326
41597CB00029B/4933